THE COMPLETE HORSESHOEING GUIDE

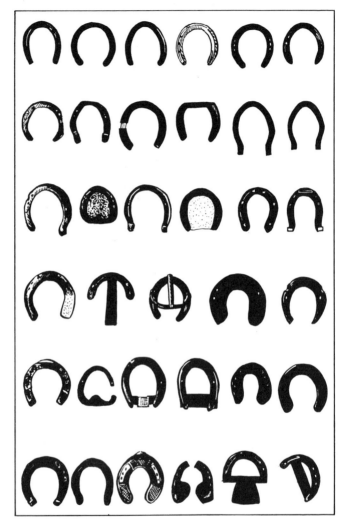

Horseshoe Variations: *This display illustrates some of the commercial, modified, and handmade shoes that can be used. There are hundreds of variations, but these shoes show the main principles involved.*

THE
COMPLETE
HORSESHOEING
GUIDE

by
Robert F. Wiseman

Norman
University of Oklahoma Press

*The paper on which this book is printed bears the watermark
of the University of Oklahoma Press and is designed to have
an effective life of at least three hundred years.*

SF
907
W6b

International Standard Book Number: 0-8061-0814-2

Library of Congress Catalog Card Number: 68-15674

I dedicate this book to my wife, who has been willing to forgo many of today's luxuries and share her husband for many long hours with horses in order that this book, which is the end result of those endeavors, may be written.

Let it be our contribution to the horse industry of the future.

Preface

THIS BOOK HAS BEEN WRITTEN for both the professional farrier and the pleasure-horse owner who wants to do his own shoeing. I have tried to present a practical book of basic principles and methods so that, after studying it, you will be able to do a normal job of shoeing without damage to the horse or his action, and can understand the reason for doing what you do. At the same time I have tried to make it as detailed and complete as possible so that it may be used as a reference.

Horseshoeing is an art and offers a real challenge to a man who loves horses and is willing to study and strive for improvement. There is always something new to learn and a better method to master. Shoeing provides pride of accomplishment, and a good farrier quickly earns the respect of those who know enough about his work to understand some of his problems. Shoeing is hard work, but once skill is attained and good equipment used, it becomes less difficult. It is said there is something about the outside of a horse that is good for the inside of a man, and the farrier knows this is true.

This book does not deal specifically with anatomy; the subject of anatomy, however, is basic to horseshoeing. Competence includes a thorough understanding of how a sound horse is put together so that an unsound one can be recognized and corrected.

Before proceeding, the reader should be aware that there are two methods of shoeing: hot and cold. In early days shoes were made from iron bars as they were needed. Later hot shoe "blanks" became available. These are heated and cut to size. At present, cold shoeing is the most common method because it requires less skill and equipment. The cold shoes available today are high-quality shoes and so cheap that it doesn't pay to make handmade shoes except when they are needed in special circumstances. Both methods of shoeing, however, are covered here.

This book had its origin in the desire to record for future generations information that is becoming lost in many parts of the country. I have based the material upon my own experience, instruction at the horseshoeing school I attended, the experience of old-time farriers, and associated reference material.

I hope you like this book.

ROBERT F. WISEMAN

Burns, Oregon

Contents

CONTENTS

Photographs
and Drawings

Charts

The Complete Horseshoeing Guide

The Anvil of God's Word

Last eve I paused beside a blacksmith's door,
    And heard the anvil ring the vesper chime;
Then looking in, I saw upon the floor,
    Old hammers worn with beating years of time.

"How many anvils have you had," said I,
    "To wear and batter all these hammers so?"
"Just one," said he, and then with twinkling eye,
    "The anvil wears the hammers out, you know."

"And so," I thought, "The Anvil of God's Word,
    For ages skeptic blows have beat upon,
Yet, though the noise of falling blows was heard,
    The anvil is unchanged, the hammers gone."

—John Clifford

Basic Principles

HOOF CARE

MUCH HAS BEEN WRITTEN on the subject of hoof care, presenting various aspects of the problem. The discussion, in this instance, will center around moisture and its influence on the health of the horse. All other factors being equal, the moisture content of the hoof will determine its qualities. Although the hoof derives some moisture from the blood, the concern here is with penetration from the outside.

The first indication that the hoof needs moisture is when the frog loses its elasticity. Later the hoof becomes hard and may develop small cracks.

The hoof will change size depending on three factors: moisture content, temperature, and soil conditions. A horse's feet may be half a size smaller in the fall after drying out during the heat of the summer. Moving a horse from hard, dry ground to soft, moist ground will help to spread the foot out. Horses raised on soft or gumbo soils may have a larger, flatter foot than is desirable.

Nature has planned that the hoof should vary in moisture content. In summer when the ground is dry and hard, the hoof also becomes dry and hard. Although this is fine for an unshod horse under normal conditions, keeping the horse in unnatural conditions and nailing a piece of iron on his foot throws nature out of balance. It then becomes necessary to see that the horse has proper care. The foot, therefore, should not be allowed to become hard and dry but should be kept moist, since the shoe is now protecting the foot.

Unless the horse is kept in a wet pasture, some provision must be made for soaking the feet. The best method is to use a "soak stall" or to put the horse periodically into a pen with a shallow water or mud floor. Filling a low box with mud or wet clay is a good method, and it is best to use warm water rather than cold. Even making the horse walk through mud to get a drink is helpful. An overflow system can be set up to keep the area around the tank wet.

After the feet are moist, and *only after* the feet are moist, may a hoof dressing be used to help the hoof retain this moisture. Most of the dressings are greasy preparations that exclude air and therefore retard evaporation. This means that they will also exclude water if applied before the feet are soaked. Be careful never to rasp the hoof wall more than necessary as this destroys the natural hoof varnish (periople) that is there to prevent evaporation. Should it be necessary to rasp the wall, a dressing may be applied to replace the varnish.

Dressing may be applied to feet that already contain the proper amount of moisture to keep them from becoming overly soft if the horse is to be used in wet surroundings.

4

Dry feet will aggravate any disease or defect of which I am aware except thrush, and, indirectly, even thrush may be aggravated through hard, contracted heels. If the horse is kept in a stall, bedding practices will determine the moisture content of the feet. If the stall is not cleaned regularly, urine will destroy the hoof varnish and make the feet vulnerable to drying. Some bedding materials, such as shavings, actually draw moisture from the feet, and, if used, the feet will have to be soaked in order to avoid harmful results.

To get an idea of how much drying affects the feet, watch a portion of wall after a horse's hoof has been trimmed. Within a few days, the ends will contract until they overlap.

Remember that "moisture is better than shoes," and a foot in good condition may not need a shoe.

Hoof Functions

The hoof has various functions that are not seen by the ordinary observer but must always be kept in mind when putting on a shoe, which at best is an unnatural elongation of the hoof wall. Anyone who attempts to shoe a horse should have at least a simple understanding of what is inside the hoof and how it works. There are many good books on this complex subject, and what is written here involves only the simplest principles.

There are four bones of primary concern: the long and short pastern bones, the angle of which determines the angle to trim the hoof; the coffin bone, which is the main bone of the foot; and the navicular bone at the rear of the foot, over which the flexor tendons slide. Under

5

these bones and seen at the heel is the plantar cushion which acts as a cushion to absorb concussion. The lateral cartilages, wings attached to the coffin bone, confine the plantar cushion and allow a proper amount of expansion. Next is the "foot skin," called the pododerm or quick, which contains blood vessels that surround and nourish the bones of the foot.

The hoof wall covers and protects these bones and tissues and also supports most of the horse's weight. Three layers make up the wall. The outer layer is a varnish-like material commonly called periople. Technically the periople extends down the hoof only three-fourths of an inch, the remainder of the hoof being covered by shiny horn scales called the *stratum tectorium*. No more of the periople than is necessary should be removed in the shoeing process, since this scaly portion prevents evaporation of moisture and drying of the hoofs.

The second layer is the horny wall itself, made of the same material as hair, and it is a nonconductor of heat or cold. It contains the pigments in colored feet.

Inside the horny wall is a layer of soft horn called the white line. Properly called the "guideline," the line can be easily distinguished from the sole by its softer texture and its laminar structure. The white line connects the sensitive tissue and the horny wall. This connection is made by insensitive laminae that intermesh with sensitive laminae and attach the wall to the coffin bone. Much of the horse's weight rests on these laminae. The white line can be seen on the bottom of the hoof between the sole and wall and indicates the shape of the foot. The shoe nails should be driven into it as much as possible.

Growing outward from the bottom of the foot is the sole. On an unshod horse the sole tends to flake off naturally, but on a shod horse the shoe allows the sole to build up. When the shoes are reset, some of the old flakes should be trimmed off.

As weight is applied to the leg and pressure is transmitted through the bones, several things happen to absorb the pressure from above and the concussion from below. The bones, especially the small ones in the knee, slide over each other slightly. The pasterns sink and the hoof expands. The frog is the key to this expansion, forming a wedge to spread the plantar cushion which then spreads the lateral cartilages. The heels contact the ground first, and this concussion helps to expand them. At the same time, the blood forms a "hydraulic cushion." This occurs thousands of times in a day's ride, and the expansion must not be hindered if the horse is to remain sound.

If the frog is cut out or kept from the ground, the plantar cushion will sink downward instead of expanding. As this occurs the lateral cartilages are pulled inward and an undesirable effect is produced. Observe an old shoe as it comes from the foot and see how the flexing of the heels has polished and worn it.

To understand the need for this expansion, consider a 1,000-pound horse. Theoretically he would carry 250 pounds on each leg. (Actually, the front legs carry more weight than the hind legs.) When in motion, however, the horse alternately transfers the weight from one leg to the opposite leg. Therefore each leg is subjected to 500 pounds of weight from above plus the shock of striking the ground from below. If the problem is considered in this way, it is remarkable that there are as many sound horses as there are.

Although the entire hoof wall grows at the same rate, the wall at the heels is the youngest since it doesn't have as far to grow. This young horn is more elastic and aids the heels in expanding.

Horseshoeing is harmful largely because it interferes with expansion. The two worst offenses are keeping the frog off the ground with heel calks and driving nails too far back in the quarters. A foot that is shod according to scientific principles will remain sound for the life of the horse.

BREEDING FOR BETTER FEET

Horses should be judged from the ground up. Nothing limits a horse as quickly as a poor foot or leg, because everything he does, he does on his feet. The main thing the breeder should remember is that the potential foal will need feet of the proper size to handle his weight. Small feet may be pretty, but they are subject to problems such as contracted heels and disease. The frog may not be large enough to act as a shock absorber and a "heart" to help pump the blood up out of the legs. Feet that are too big will cause the horse to be clumsy and slow. If the foot has a normal shape, it will not break down as quickly, even though small, as one with an abnormal shape.

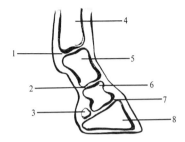

BONES OF PASTERN AND FOOT

1—*Fetlock joint*
2—*Pastern joint*
3—*Navicular bone*
4—*Cannon bone*

5—*Long pastern bone*
6—*Short pastern bone*
7—*Coffin joint*
8—*Coffin bone*

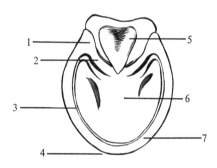

BOTTOM VIEW OF HORSE'S FOOT

1—*Buttress*
2—*Bar*
3—*White line*
4—*Toe*

5—*Frog*
6—*Sole*
7—*Wall*

Note: The white line is located between the wall and the sole and is the true indicator of the shape of the hoof. This is where the nails should be driven.

Many defects such as splints, spavins, hock deformities, and conformation deformities are congenital, and they, or the tendency to develop the defect, may be passed from parent to offspring. Environmental factors such as nutrition and use will have a great deal to do with whether these defects occur, but why start out with the odds against you?

Other things to watch for in addition to hoof size are these: hoof angle, thickness of wall, quality of horn, and shape of feet. Do not breed two horses having these same types of abnormalities. Thickness of the hoof wall seems to correspond to the thickness of the horse's skin. Keep this in mind when shoeing purebred horses as the wall is often thin, and the shoe must be fitted carefully.

If a stud has to be shod during the breeding season, shoe his front feet short with well-trimmed heels. Don't use calks on the hind feet of a mare that is to be bred or she may injure the stud.

One of the greatest potentials for improving horses, which should not be overlooked, is breeding for better feet. It is certainly easier to shoe a horse having a good normal foot, and the horseshoer will be grateful. The object is not so much trying to improve poor feet but trying to raise horses that don't need improvement.

How to Judge Hoof Quality

First of all, do not confuse a hardened condition from lack of moisture with a tough, good-quality hoof.

A good hoof will be of the proper size to handle the horse's weight and will have a good shape. Normally the front feet are rounded and the hind feet are pointed. The outside half of the hoof will be slightly fuller and the wall will have more slope. In other words, the shape of the left and right feet is distinct.

In an average-size horse the wall should be about three-eighths to one-half inch thick at the toe and become thinner toward the heels to allow the heels to expand. The hoof should be smooth, free from rings, and covered with a natural varnish. The underside of the foot should have a concave sole, large healthy frog, well-developed bars to help support the wall, and horn of proper thickness, as mentioned above. (Of all the horses I have worked with, only one has had hoof walls that I thought were too thick.) A solid black foot will be of better quality than an unpigmented white foot, although white feet may be of good quality if all four are white.

ALTERATION OF THE FOOT

Despite the assertions of some authors to the contrary, the shape and size of the foot can be altered through the shoeing process. This can be done more readily with a young horse than with an older one. The basic principle involved is the blood supply. If one side of the hoof receives more blood, that side will grow faster. A crooked hoof can be helped by the use of counterirritants applied at the coronet on the lower side. If the wall is mistakenly left too high on one side while the horse is being shod (foot broken "in" or "out"), the high side will receive more blood, and a shoe will keep the wall from wearing away naturally. Eventually a crooked foot

11

will be the result. (See the illustration, "Faults of Trimming," in Chapter V.)

If the hoof is flared and overexpanded, it can be narrowed by rasping the flares during each shoeing, limiting expansion by the use of nails far back in the quarters and heels, and keeping the frog off of the ground. The hoof may be expanded, when necessary, by one of the methods covered in Chapter IX under "Contracted Heels."

When the feet are twisted, the prominent side can be made slightly lower than the scant side. The blood supply, therefore, will be increased to the side that was originally low, causing it to lengthen under treatment. Trimming the feet out of balance in this manner is a drastic measure and should not be done on mature horses or horses older than two years.

How Often to Reshoe

All of the books I have read about horseshoeing recommend resetting the shoes every five or six weeks. I usually disagree with this belief. In my opinion, the length of time between shoeings depends on several factors and can range from five to ten weeks. The rate of growth varies with age, moisture content, diet, and temperature. The way in which the horse will be used is also a factor. A horse shod with short heels will need his shoes reset more often than a horse shod long in the heels. There is no advantage in resetting the shoes until necessary as harm is done to the hoof by making new holes in the horn. Conversely, allowing too much time to elapse is worse than resetting the shoes too often. Each case is different, and it will pay to determine what is right for your horse and then stick with it.

If you have a good farrier, you can give him the "go-ahead" to take care of the horse and stop worrying. The farrier will keep a record and make appointments at the proper time. The skill with which the shoes are attached will greatly determine when they should be reset. When regarded in this way, a first-class farrier may be cheap at his price.

As the shoe wears down, it will bend or break easily. The nailheads will also wear down until there is not enough head to hold the shoe. If the shoe is bent out, it could cut the opposite leg. If it is bent in, it could press on the sole, crushing the sensitive tissues and causing a bruise. In addition, broken nails in the branch may puncture the sole.

If the shoe stays on and does not bend, it keeps the wall from breaking away normally, and the hoof will grow extremely long. As the wall grows down and forward, the hoof eventually will grow out from under the horse and will not support his weight as it should. A strain is put on the tendons and ligaments at the rear of the leg. Reshoeing a horse in this condition is such a drastic change that he will be sore for a few days, especially at the front of the pastern where the extensor tendons are located.

When a horse is not in use or does not need shoes, let him go bare. This is nature's way and the best way. Use "horse" sense when it comes to resetting your horse's shoes, but at the same time remember that the war was lost "for lack of a nail."

13

Handling the Feet

There are two methods of shoeing. The first is to prepare all four feet before setting the shoes, and the second is to prepare a foot and then fit and nail a shoe on it. I prefer the first method, because using the same set of tools as you work around the horse saves time. The horse becomes used to being handled all around before you start nailing and will accept the jarring better. You may find something, such as opposite feet of different sizes, that will influence the way each foot is shod; and if the shoe is already on when such a problem is discovered, it will be too late.

It is not always possible to use this method. If the horse's hoof is very tender for any reason, the shoe may have to be set before he will put his weight on that foot so that you can work on the opposite side. If the hoofs are dry and brittle, you may want to shoe them immediately after trimming in order to avoid breakage while trimming the other feet.

When picking up the feet, always make your actions slow and deliberate. *Be sure the horse knows where you are.* As you face to the rear of the horse, touch him with your shoulder, then slide your hand down his leg. Pat the leg above the hoof a few times and say, "O.K." This gives the horse a chance to pick the hoof up himself and is good psychology. If he does not pick it up himself, you will have to push him slightly off balance with your shoulder to take his weight off of that leg. Use the same procedure in working with the hind foot, but stand for-

Making a Horseshoe in the Shop

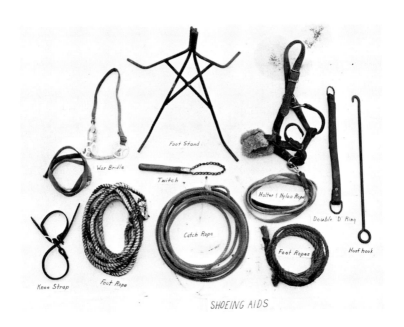

War Bridle

Foot Stand

Twitch

Halter & Nylon Rope

Double 'D' Ring

Hoof hook

Catch Rope

Knee Strap

Foot Rope

Foot Ropes

SHOEING AIDS

Shoeing Aids

How to Hold the Front Foot

How to Hold the Hind Foot

Using a Hoof Gauge to Determine Angle

Using the Knee Strap

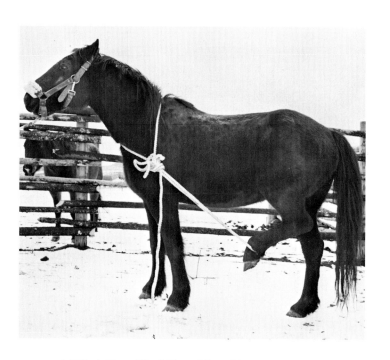

A Hind Foot Tied Up with a "Scotch Hobble"

A Horse Tied Down: *This photograph shows the method of tying the feet together, the use of a hay bale to hold the feet in the working position, and the method of holding the horse's head.*

ward toward his head as far as possible so that if he kicks forward, he will miss you. Put one hand on his hip so if he should try to kick, you can push him off balance. Now slide the other hand down his leg, grasp the leg low, and pull it forward. Move in closely and, grasping the leg with both hands, pull the hoof back where you want it in order to work on it. *Always keep the toe tipped up.* I cannot stress this too much. With the toe tipped up, he will have a much harder time jerking away from you, and with your arm locked over the hock and the toe bent up, you can hold most horses if the head is tied short.

Let the leg hang as naturally as possible and avoid putting a strain on it, or the horse will try to jerk away. Many horses that had to be thrown before can be shod in a standing position by the use of this method.

Never allow a horse to throw his weight on you. It may be necessary to tie one leg up and make him learn to balance on three legs. Do not permit the horse to put his foot down, but, instead, put it down for him when you are through. Say, "O.K.," just as you do.

WHAT IS A GOOD JOB?

A good job is what is right for a particular horse. It may look different or odd to the horse owner, and the farrier will want to explain the "why" of it. This is one business, however, when the "customer is not always right," and a good farrier will do what is best for the horse or will not do the job at all. The main points to observe are listed on the following pages.

15

Type of Shoe

The type and material of the shoe must correspond with the way in which the horse will be used. Remember that a plate shoe is best, and there must be a reason for using calks (these points are discussed in greater detail later in the book). The same is true of weight—use the lightest shoe that will do the job.

Shape

The shoe should correspond to the natural shape of the horse's foot as shown by the white line, and this generally means rounded shoes on the front feet and pointed ones on the back feet. Make certain that the toes are not dubbed off to fit a shoe that is not formed for the foot. Each pair of feet should be of the same size and the same angle.

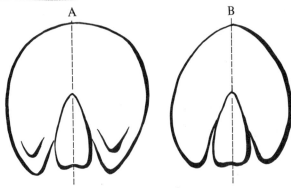

NORMAL FOOT SHAPE

Bottom view of right front foot showing fullness of outside half—Note the rounded toe.

Bottom view of right hind foot—Note the pointed toe.

Condition of Hoof

The two most important considerations are that the hoof be balanced (wall trimmed the same on both sides) and level. In order to check the balance, lead the horse onto a level surface and observe the foot from the front when he is standing on it squarely.

Check from the side to make sure the angle corresponds to that of the pastern and that the heels of opposite feet are trimmed to the same height. Pick up the foot to make sure that it is level; there should be no extra rasping or smoothing of the wall. If possible, the frog should touch the ground when the shoe is on, or if this is not possible, at least it should not be pared away. The bars should not be cut out, but simply made level with the wall.

Fit

Once the foot has been balanced and leveled, the shoe must be fitted to it. The shoe should fit tightly, with no air spaces between the wall and the shoe, and should not rest on the sole. Old flakes should be trimmed from the sole and the *sole lowered slightly between the wall and the bars to prevent corns*. The shoe may be very slightly wider at the heels than the hoof in order to support the wall at the heels as they expand; however, this will vary among different horses. (See "Flat Foot and Overexpansion" in Chapter X.)

Nailing

The nails should be driven high enough to give a good hold and still have almost their full width to form a strong clinch. Nails should not be driven where they would interfere with normal expansion. The clinches should all be the same height (about three-fourths of an inch), so that as the foot grows, the holes will be cut out and not interfere with subsequent shoeings. The clinches should be well seated and smooth. No more nails than necessary should be used. A normal foot has six nails per shoe, the two toe holes being reserved for instances when one or more of the nails cannot be driven because of cracks or broken walls. These holes will be available for frost nails in the winter.

Abnormalities:

If there is anything unusual or wrong with the foot, it should be taken care of. A good job will stop cracks and make the horse usable or aid healing if he is lame. A good job of shoeing will generally make the hoof break over center and fly straight. In other words, if a horse needs a squared toe, a lateral extension, a trailer, or a clip, it will be there.

HIS FIRST SET OF SHOES

The colt's first set of shoes is as much a part of his training as is the riding. If done properly, shoeing will help all phases of the training as he finds out that he is not being harmed, but must submit to man's will. A colt whose feet hurt will not learn much.

If the colt has been brought in for the first time, he will consider himself a "victim for torture" and do everything he can to get away. If the colt is frightened and hurt at this time, future shoeings will require extra

18

work. Considering the number of times he will be shod during his life, it pays to spend some extra time initially.

Giving the colt a good start not only makes him easier to shoe, but will teach him to trust and "like" people. Such horses are easy to catch and willing to do their best for their owners, whereas a horse that was mistreated as a colt will probably always do his best to avoid associating with those two-legged creatures who abuse him. I would much rather put the first set of shoes on a colt than to shoe an old, spoiled saddle horse that knows all the tricks for "foiling the manicurist."

It is best to handle the colt enough so that he will not have to have his legs tied for his first shoeing; this makes the process easier for everyone. If he must be tied, be sure to pad the rope or use a strap. The colt will be more difficult to shoe in the future if he is abused, and he will remember the person who mishandled him. A long memory doesn't only occur in an elephant.

A good time to shoe a colt is after his first extensive ride, since he will be a little tired and likely to stand better. Before starting work, be sure that the nail holes are clean and the nails fit easily. Try to avoid hitting the shoe with the hammer, for hard pounding will convey shock to the pastern and the colt will try to jerk away. To get the colt used to having his hind legs handled, reach back and rub and pat his hind leg before putting the front foot down.

Often the smallest shoe available will be too large for a colt. In this case, cut off the heels, cutting each branch at a 45° angle so that the outside is longer, and smooth them with a file or grinder. If very much is cut off, don't use the rear nail holes as they will be too far back in the hoof, limiting expansion. Instead, use the front three holes on each side. A colt's hoof wall is thin; therefore the shoe *must* be fitted so that the holes lie over the white line. Be careful not to aim the nails too high.

Use the lightest shoe that will do the job and avoid calks. A colt does not have an established "way of going," and heavy shoes could throw him out of stride and tire him out, both of which could lead to a wreck. Rolling the outer edge around the entire toe will let the foot break over in any direction.

Locating Lameness

A horse is a complex mechanism, and when something goes wrong it is not always easy to determine which part, or combination of parts, is responsible for the trouble. Finding the trouble as quickly as possible is important so that treatment may be started while it will still be effective.

Try to discover if anything has happened to the horse recently that could possibly have caused the problem. Consider conformation and to what difficulties it could predispose the horse. Remember that most lameness occurs in the feet, or at least below the knee, and that the front feet are more susceptible than the hind feet.

In case of lameness, it must be determined whether the lameness comes from the bone, muscles, tendons, or ligaments, and whether the soreness is in the front, the back, or both areas. A thorough examination should be made in a place familiar to the horse and without any distractions. Do not assume that, because there is an obvious swelling, the swelling is the cause, or the only cause, of lameness. Keep in mind that the horse could have injured another area in an attempt to protect the original injury.

Before starting the examination, watch the horse move by himself; look for any indication that he is trying to keep weight off of one leg. A normal horse will stand so that his weight is evenly distributed on his feet and there is no strain on the tendons.

If the lameness is in front, the head and hip will dip when the sound foot strikes the ground during a trot. When standing, the horse may have his hind feet under him as far as possible in order to take weight off the front legs. He may also "point" the lame leg or hold it out in front.

If the lameness is in back, the hock of the sound leg will rise higher and dip lower than that of the lame one during the trot. The head may drop as the lame foot strikes the ground in order to take some of the weight from it. The hip will drop toward the sound side. The hind quarters will move to the sound side "dog fashion," because the stride of the affected side is shorter. (In the gallop the body is naturally canted because the leading leg takes a longer stride.) Observe the horse from behind to check for hip indications; at rest the horse will "point" the foot.

If he is lame in all four feet, the horse will not want to move, and if he must, he will take short, stilty steps. If he is lame in both forelegs, the head may not drop at all.

Next feel the feet and legs from the shoulder down

for any swelling, heat, tenderness, or lack of sensation, and compare opposite legs with each other.

If the horse is shod, it is best to remove the shoes. If you can't do this, tap each nail with a hammer and watch for any indication of pain.

Clean the hoof and listen to see if the pick strikes metal. Explore any black spots, red areas, or cuts in the sole and frog. Most difficulties occur in the hoof itself, even though they may seem to be located elsewhere. If the blood vessels are full and pulsing along the leg and fetlock, suspect the hoof. If everything looks normal on the outside, check the inside by applying pressure. This can be done by tapping the hoof with a hammer or, better, with the use of "hoof testers" as described in Chapter II. Of course, X rays are available from a veterinarian, who can also use a stethoscope to discover any unusual noise while the hoof is being flexed.

Now take the horse to a smooth, hard, level area and watch him walk and trot. Make him back up; if he has trouble, bone spavin, stringhalt, or hip, shoulder, or stifle lameness can be suspected (see Chapter IX).

Have someone whom the horse knows lead him or ride him, giving him plenty of lead rope or rein so that his head is free. Watch for the head, hip, and hock actions described earlier. Watch for abnormalities of gait, such as stubbing the toe (in a normal horse the heels strike first), trying to walk on the inside or outside of the hoof, or landing with *all* the weight on the heel. Compare the rise, fall, and swing of each foot. Listen to the hoofbeats, since the sound hoof strikes the ground harder than the lame one.

Turn the horse sharply to see if he hesitates or turns differently on one side than the other. If lameness worsens going downhill, suspect the heels; if lameness worsens going uphill, suspect the toes.

Lead the horse over an obstacle, and if he has difficulty, his shoulder, hip, or stifle may be the cause. A rectal examination should be made if a hip or pelvic injury is suspected. Pull the leg out away from the body to test for pain in the shoulder or hip. Push against the hip; if the horse resists but finally hops on his sound leg, suspect spavin or stifle. Indications of shoulder lameness are:

1. Lifting the head when the leg is advanced
2. Foot lifted only slightly above the ground
3. Short stride
4. Stumbling
5. Restricted movement of shoulder joint
6. Indifference to hardness of ground
7. Swinging the leg outward to bring it forward without moving the shoulder.

If lameness has been present for some time, a shrinking of the shoulder muscles above the lame leg may be noticeable as the horse has not used this leg as much as the others. This condition is called "sweeny."

If the lameness has not been located by this time, work the horse until he is hot, let him stand until he has cooled off, and then repeat the procedure. This will generally make the lameness more apparent.

A final test is to lather the horse's shoulder and leg

with soap. After several hours the soap may still be moist over the inflamed area as the increased temperature keeps the soap soft while it dries elsewhere. To make this test, dissolve three heaping tablespoons of strong yellow laundry soap and one level teaspoon of salt in a half pint of warm water to form a lather. Exercise the horse enough to aggravate the lameness, then apply the lather and wait for results.

Since the horse is lame because of pain, the veterinarian may be able to locate the injured area by blocking nerves with a local anesthetic until the horse is without pain. This method is easier with acute pain than with sporadic or recurrent pain.

The above are general tests to locate lameness. Once it has been narrowed down to one or two areas, further information and specific tests can be found under the appropriate pathological or physical defect headings in this book. For instance, if you suspect the hock, look under "Spavin, Curb, Thoroughpin," etc., in Chapter IX. In addition, does lameness increase or decrease with use? See "Lameness Indicators: I" for possible causes.

LAMENESS INDICATORS: I

If the horse:

Warms out of lameness, suspect

      Muscular structures
      Tendons, ligaments, and cartilage
      Arthritic joints
      Bone spavin
      Ringbone

Stringhalt
Navicular

Worsens with use, suspect
Splints
Curb
Azoturia (metabolic toxin)
Worm larvae interfering with circulation
Note: Cases of long standing may react differently.

LAMENESS INDICATORS: II

Indicator	*Suspect*
Drops head when left front foot contacts ground	Right front leg
Drops head when right front foot contacts ground	Left front leg
Drops head when left hind foot contacts ground	Left hind leg
Drops head when right hind foot contacts ground	Right hind leg
Drops right hip	Left hind leg
Drops left hip	Right hind leg
Walks on toe	Navicular, ringbone on rear of pastern
Walks on heel	Founder, sidebones, ringbone on front of pastern, rheumatism, seedy toe, wall tumor, toe crack, dropped sole
Has trouble backing	Bone spavin, stifle, shoulder lameness
Lame on hard ground	Feet

| Lame on soft ground | Shoulder or stifle |
| Points toe | Pointed foot or limb |

Note: Use this chart in a general way only, as more than one factor may be involved.

WEIGHT

Weighted shoes are useful in many cases; however, they do not always give the desired results and generally should be used only as a last resort. Often the advantage gained by special shoes is lost because of the added weight. Weight, no matter how it is applied, always increases fatigue and decreases speed and agility. It also increases length of stride, radius of arc and delays take-off of the foot. Weight as used in special cases, such as trotting horses and gaited horses, is covered under the respective headings in Chapter XI.

Some men, having so much faith in toe weights, will guarantee that, on a horse shod in this way, the front quarters will run so fast that wheels must be put under the hind feet so that they can keep up; and in a three-mile race, the front quarters will reach the stables in time to feed on a peck of oats before the hind quarters catch up.

Horses, especially young ones that are not confirmed in their gaits, will sometimes interfere or forge as a result of the added weight (see Chapter X under the appropriate subtitle).

The lightest shoe that will allow the horse to get the job done should always be used. A light shoe protects as well as a heavy one and may last longer. Remember

26

that "an ounce at the toe means a pound at the withers."

To understand the principle of weight, we must consider the leg as if it were simply suspended. When the horse is in action, these rules are modified somewhat. Weight added to the inside of a suspended hoof will tend to push the hoof to the outside and vice versa. Weight added to the heels will tend to push the toe forward. When the foot is put in action, however, the weight in the heels is acted upon by inertia and when the hoof is picked up will tend to raise the heels. Many old-time shoers added weight to the outside of the shoe to stop interfering, claiming to have had luck with this method.

Here are some rules of weight: Weight on the horse's back (the rider) causes a longer stride. Weight in the heels of the hind shoe increases action of the hock, and heavy front shoes increase the action of the forequarters. Weight in the heels tends to increase the height of the first half of the stride, while weight in the toe tends to increase the height of the last half. A heavy shoe may increase the length of the stride depending on factors affecting the breakover, the freshness of the horse, and whether or not the foot wings in or out.

Each horse is different and some experimenting will probably need to be done in order to find out how the horse can be helped most. Use bell boots until the proper remedy is discovered. I think that the horse with flexible, loose joints may be helped by the addition of weight where another horse would not be. Remember, if it can be done some other way, *don't* use weight.

The accompanying chart shows the weight of iron of various sizes in ounces per lineal inch of stock.

27

Weight of Iron
(in ounces)

Width in inches	Thickness		
	$5/16$	$3/8$	$1/2$
$3/4$	1.06	1.27	1.71
1	1.41	1.77	2.27
$1\frac{1}{4}$	1.77	2.12	2.55
$1\frac{1}{2}$	2.12	2.55	3.40
2	2.84	3.40	4.53

As an example, if you wanted a twenty-four-ounce shoe when you were finished and wanted to make it out of 2-inch by $3/8$-inch iron, the calculation would be as follows:

$$24.00 \div 3.40 = 7.1 \text{ inches}$$

The stock might be cut slightly longer to allow for trimming the heels.

Now draw out the iron to make a shoe that will fit the horse, and weight can be left at the toe, on either side, or at the heels.

Hoof Angle

Generally the angle of the hoof should be the same as that of the pastern and shoulder. There must be a deviation from this rule in special cases. Books on horseshoeing give the angle of the front feet as 45–50 degrees and that of the hind feet as 50–55 degrees. I do not like to set limits to degrees because horses and the way they will be used vary greatly. Many horses go very well with

28

a smaller angle behind than in front. Trim the foot to the natural angle of the pastern. Angle can be measured by a special foot gauge.

The steeper the angle, the quicker the foot will break over. This is the reason the toe of the front foot is lowered when trying to keep a horse from forging, while the heels of the hind feet are lowered. When training a horse to come to a sliding stop, a lower angle will help the horse to shoot his hind feet under him.

Angle must be disregarded in conditions such as navicular disease when the heels are built up to help the horse walk on his toes. This is true of injuries to the tendons as well.

Horses with normal feet will have the best balance and action when shod at the natural angle of the pasterns, and this varies with each individual.

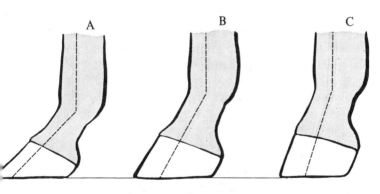

ANGLE OF PASTERNS

Sloping pastern   *Average pastern*   *Stumpy pastern*

All of the above pastern conformations can be called normal for an individual horse. When shoeing, observe the normal angle, and whenever possible, apply a shoe that will maintain this angle. Each type has some advantages and disadvantages. Horses with sloping pasterns are smooth to ride because the pasterns cushion the ride in the same way as springs under a car. The average angle, however, gives the best results in the long run because it offers the best combination of strength and springiness.

SAFETY

There are many things you can do in addition to keeping your insurance paid.

1. Have a clean area, with no obstructions, to work in.
2. Pick out your "accidents waiting to happen" and remove or correct them before they occur.
3. Keep all ropes and equipment in good shape.
4. Never get in a place where you can't "get away."
5. Bend or twist off each nail as soon as it is driven. If you bend them over to cut later, cut the nails on the side toward yourself first.
6. Do not let other horses into the area where you are working.
7. Try to work where the horse can look around and will not be suddenly startled.
8. Wear fairly close-fitting clothes.
9. Gloves will protect your hands from the rasp and nails.

10. Always wear a good apron or chaps when nailing. Have long strings on your apron so you can cross them behind and tie in front. Do not have leg ties. Arranged in this manner, the apron can be jerked off if the horse hooks a nail in it.

11. Hard-toed boots with flat heels are the best foot-gear.

12. A cap will protect your head from being "scalped" if you are bitten.

13. Work smoothly and deliberately. Make sure the horse knows where you are at all times. Hurry when you can, but not when near the horse.

14. Act as if you did not expect the horse to hurt you in any way, and he probably won't.

15. Learn how to work in close to a horse. If he kicks you, he will push more than hit, and you will be able to get in close to his shoulder to avoid his feet if he strikes. When holding the hoof on your knee, keep your knee bent so that, if the horse puts all his weight on you, you can let his hoof slip off instead of losing your knee cap.

16. If the horse gets mad while you are driving the nails, step away from him before releasing the foot.

17. Be prepared; always try to prevent the wrong thing from happening.

II.

Tools—Their Care and Use

I T IS POSSIBLE to start shoeing horses with only a small investment in the basic tools and to add more equipment as skill and need require. Horseshoeing tools are designed for a specific purpose; many tools that are suitable for blacksmith work are not suitable for shoeing horses. Tools and their condition are a very good indication of the kind of work a man will do. "A mechanic is known by the tools he uses."

Shoes and tools are usually available at saddle and hardware stores. In the last few years several new manufacturers have entered the field and their products are very good. High-quality material, good craftsmanship, and scientific principles are combined to produce excellent shoes and tools. Catalogs are available for the necessary equipment.

Tools will be discussed under three headings: Shoeing Tools, Metalworking Tools, and Miscellaneous.

SHOEING TOOLS

Anvil

A farrier's anvil should be used. Farriers' anvils are

32

narrow at the arch end and have a large, tapered horn. Many also have a projection that is used when drawing clips. Some anvils have a flat area, or chipping block, used for cutting so that the face will not be damaged.

Mount the anvil on a heavy block so that, as you stand with your arm hanging down and your hand closed, your knuckles will touch the face. The horn of the anvil should point toward the left for a right-handed man. When working with a hard-surfaced shoe, do not hammer the hardened area against the anvil face.

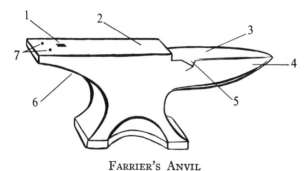

FARRIER'S ANVIL

1—*Hole for hardy*	4—*Horn*
2—*Face*	5—*Projection for drawing clips*
3—*Chipping block*	6—*Arch*
7—*Pritchel Holes*	

If children get dangerously near, put a little water on the anvil, drop a wide piece of white-hot metal on it, and say, "If you don't look out, somebody's going to get hurt around here," just as you hit the metal with a hammer. The resulting noise will encourage children to stay at a safe distance.

33

Hoof Nippers

Nippers are used to cut off the excess wall. There are two types, one with two sharp jaws and the other with one sharp and one flat jaw, commonly called a hoof parer. Both cut from the inside of the hoof toward the outside. I prefer the double-edged nipper as there is no problem in getting the flat edge on the outside, and a good, clean cut is made all the way through.

Before starting to work, remove all nail stubs and clean out dirt and grit in order to keep the nipper sharp. Begin on the low heel and work around the toe, breaking the horn loose as you go. Hold the nipper so that it makes a flat cut and not one that tapers toward the outside or toward the toe. For a smoother surface, let the old cut be a guide instead of making a completely new cut each time. Touch the cutting edges with a file occasionally to make the work easier.

Hoof Knife

This knife comes with a wooden or metal handle, and some knives have a blade that pulls in or folds up. A hoof knife is used to remove tags from the frog and lower the sole when necessary. It is often used to clean the hoof, but in order to keep the knife sharp, use a pick for this purpose.

To sharpen the knife, grind it on a fine stone if necessary. Follow this procedure by using a fine mill file and whetstone. Always sharpen *toward* the cutting edge (this is a basic rule of sharpening). Small round files and specially shaped whetstones are available for sharpening the curved end. Keep the knife in a leather scabbard so

34

that it does not come in contact with other metal. Some farriers sharpen an area on top of the blade, but this is a matter of preference.

Sole Knife

A horse that has been unshod during very dry weather will have a sole that is so hard it cannot be cut with a hoof knife. If the sole should have to be cut for any reason, a dish-shaped sole knife, hit with a hammer, will do the job.

To make the dish-shaped knife, take a piece of automotive leaf spring and cut out the pattern. Heat to a light red and bend the cutting edge into a spoon shape. Grind the bottom until it is sharp and temper the edge as described in Chapter VII. This is actually a chisel more than a knife as it cuts when hit with a hammer.

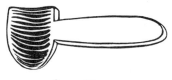

SOLE KNIFE

Rasp

Because of the high price of rasps and the extra time and work involved when using a dull one, their use and care should be discussed here. Although a rasp can be sharpened, it should be kept sharp as long as possible. Never let the teeth touch other metal. When using the rasp, don't bear down too hard but let it "float," and try to rasp from the center outward. Keep the rasp in a leather pouch, and when laying it down, be sure the teeth are up. If the rasp becomes wet, dry it off so that it will not rust. Keep two rasps on hand, one for shaping the foot and an older one for trimming the hoof after the shoe has been attached. The best way to keep the rasp sharp is to develop skill with the nippers, since their use will cut down the amount of rasping necessary.

There are two main types from which to choose: the tanged rasp, having teeth slanted one direction, and the divided rasp, having teeth slanted in opposite directions from the middle. Rasps also vary in thickness, weight, and tooth size. I prefer a heavy, tanged rasp with large teeth for general work. The tang may be taped or inserted in a wooden handle for more comfortable and easy use. Some rasps can be sharpened and some cannot. If the rasp will be sharpened later, be sure to buy one with the teeth set in rows, instead of alternated, so that they can be filed a row at a time.

The objectives of sharpening are to remove the temper from the teeth so that a file can cut them in order to sharpen the teeth and then to harden them again. This process takes time, but I generally save all of my dull rasps during the summer and sharpen them in the winter. To remove the temper, heat the teeth until they are red-hot and let them cool slowly. This can be done with an oxyacetylene flame or a forge. If a forge is used, do not cover the rasp with coals but hold it above the fire until the teeth are red-hot. Now, a tapered mill file or small, three-cornered file that will fit between the teeth is needed. Touch the underside of each tooth lightly, then file the top until the tooth is sharp. To harden the teeth, heat over a clean fire until they are an even red color, being very careful never to burn the teeth. Quickly dip the rasp in oil or salt water, and move it back and forth endwise in the liquid until cooled. Test the hardness with a sharp file; the teeth should be so hard that the file will not cut them with ordinary pressure. The rasp itself may vary in hardness depending on the heating temperature, but if the teeth are sharp and hard, the rasp will serve you well.

A final thought on rasps—never hit a horse with a rasp unless you are wearing gloves. Your blood will rust the rasp.

Hammers

Two types of hammers are used in actual shoeing, the nailing hammer and the fitting hammer. The nailing hammer is used for driving nails; some farriers also use the claws for wringing off the nails. Keep an extra handle for the hammer in your outfit as it can be easily broken if stepped on. You will appreciate a good nailing hammer if you ever have to finish a job with a blacksmith's hammer.

The fitting hammer is used to bend and shape the shoe. This hammer weighs about three pounds, while a nailing hammer weighs no more than one pound.

Clinchers

Clinchers are a special type of tongs fitted with teeth; one jaw fits against the nailhead while the other bends the nail end to form the clinch. Clinches should be tapped down with the hammer after forming the clinch to make a smooth surface. Clinching can be done with a hammer, but clinchers make the job a little easier.

37

Clinching Block

A piece of one-inch square iron about three inches long works well for drawing up the nails. The clinching block is held against the clinch while the nailheads are tapped. Sometimes the nippers are held under the clinch. A variation of this is to build up one side of the nippers so that they are flat, as shown in the accompanying illustration.

Keep the jaw cool while welding as too much heat will remove the temper and put the jaws out of alignment.

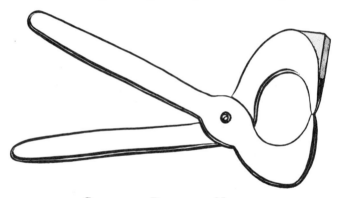

CLINCHING BLOCK ON NIPPERS

Buffer

The buffer, also known as a "clinch cutter," is used to cut or straighten the clinches so that the nails can be removed. Commercial tools usually have one sharp end to drive nail stubs from the shoes, etc. The best buffer I have used is made from half of a hoof nipper; the handle is simply bent back as shown in the accompanying illustration.

38

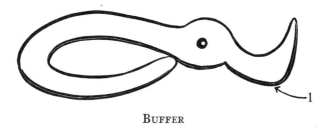

BUFFER

1—*Hammer here*

Forepunch

The forepunch has a point the size of the nailhead and is used to countersink the hot iron so that the nail-head will sit in the hole and not be completely worn off. A pritchel is then used to complete the hole.

Pritchel

A pritchel is used to open and clean nail holes. It is a good idea to hold the shoe up to the light and check the holes before starting to nail the shoe on, as it is embarrassing to drive nails only to find that a hole or two cannot be used. The point of the pritchel should be kept sharp and flat in order to cut out the burr. It should be the same size as the nail being driven when measured two-thirds of the way up the shank. It is necessary to have a pritchel for each nail size, and each can be numbered with a metal stamp to correspond with the nail numbers. Never let the pritchel become red-hot when using it on a hot shoe or the temper will be lost, and the tool will bend and thicken. Cool it in water when necessary.

The pritchel should be driven from the bottom of the shoe in the same way as the nail is driven. If it is driven from the hoof side, "back pritcheling," the burrs will remain and weaken and cut the nails. If you have a round pritchel, flatten the handle the same way that the point is flattened so that it is not necessary to look at the point each time.

A good holder for pritchels and punches can be made by welding a pipe shut at the bottom and putting some wax inside. The points can be put in the wax for protection after they are cool.

If you do not have a pritchel and need to clean a hole that is burred over, take a nail that corresponds to the hole size, cut it off, leaving the head and one-third of the length, and drive this into the hole to clean it.

Pull-off Tongs

These tongs are used to grasp the shoe and pry it loose when it is being removed. Be careful not to put too much pressure on the sole as the sensitive parts could be bruised or crushed.

Nail Cutter

A nail cutter is used to cut off the nail points, giving a neater job than can be obtained by wringing the points with the hammer claws. A ten-inch nipper is good for this work.

Apron

An apron can save a lot of torn pants and hide. It should be made of thick leather, and the tie strings should be long enough to be crossed behind and tied

40

in front. The apron should not fasten around the legs. If a horse hooks the nails of his shoe through the leather and starts using you as a ping pong ball, all you need to do is jerk the bow in front, and you will fly clear. Pockets can be sewed on the apron for the knife and hoof pick.

Hoof Pick

A hoof pick is used to clean the feet, especially the clefts beside the frog. It can be made in a few minutes and will help to keep your knife sharp.

HOOF PICK
(*Over-all length 5½″*)

It is a good idea to paint the handles of the small tools red so that they will show up easily if covered with straw, etc.

Divider

This tool is used to measure from the top of the hoof to the toe, making certain that opposite feet are of equal length. It is also used to take measurements of the hoof when making special shoes.

41

Metalworking Tools

Forge

Many horseshoers do not own a forge, thus limiting the work they can do. Cold shoes can be bent enough to fit normal feet, but heat is required for any unusual circumstances.

Blacksmith coal differs from regular coal in that it changes to coke. A high-quality coal can be easily broken in the fingers. A fire is banked with wet coal, and as the gases are driven off, coke is formed, which burns cleanly. Charcoal can be used for heating fine tool steel. If the fire is to be left untended for a few minutes, the slide should be opened to allow air into the fire to keep the flame from dying out. A piece of wood put in the fire and covered with charcoal will also help to keep the fire burning. A crater of cement or firebrick around the twyer (tuyère) ball helps to make a good fire.

A fire shovel, fire rake, and an assortment of tongs for different sizes of iron (a long-handled pair for holding shoes or tools in the fire and a short-handled pair, preferably adjustable, for holding the shoe as it is being worked on) are also required at the forge. Coal may be kept in a tilted garbage can so that it can be removed easily.

Hardy

A hardy is used in the anvil to cut and bend hot iron; the center of an iron bar can be located by balancing it on the hardy. It has a square stem that fits into the hole in the anvil face. The stem should extend through the bottom of the anvil so that the hardy can be tapped out if it sticks.

A half-round hardy is very useful for trimming the heels of a hot shoe (see accompanying illustration). Some men prefer the bevel on the inside.

HALF-ROUND HARDY

Rounding Hammer

This hammer, used for making shoes and drawing clips, has one flat face and one rounded one. A two-and-one-half-pound hammer is recommended. The rounded face is used for drawing out clips and "seating out" the shoe so that the sole will not bear on it; the flat face is used for leveling the shoe.

Crease Cutter

This tool is also called a "fullering iron" and is used to make a crease about two-thirds of the shoe depth for the nailheads or to repair a damaged crease in a keg shoe. This tool can be used instead of the forepunch mentioned earlier in this chapter.

To make the crease cutter, take a piece of one-inch-square steel, bend it slightly, and cut out a portion so

43

that there is a rim that will make the crease when the tool is driven into the hot iron. The rim should be deepest in the center so that the tool can be rocked to form a tapered crease. Weld a handle to the block and temper it at a purple color.

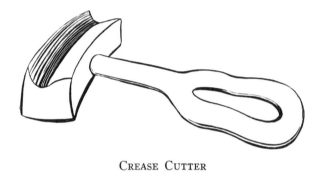

CREASE CUTTER

Vise

The vise is useful for many things, such as hot-rasping the heels and turning calks. Some vises are equipped with a strong spring to close the jaws instead of a turn-screw, and these are faster and more efficient when handling hot iron. A piece from a rasp welded to the jaw will give a firm grip.

Gas Welding Outfit

If small gas bottles are used, the welding outfit can be carried with you and will be very handy. In addition to welding on extensions, applying borium, etc., the outfit can take the place of a forge. It is a good idea to have a separate tool box for carrying welding rod, scratchers, dark goggles, and tips. Some farriers cut extensions and calks before they are needed and then weld them on as the situation requires.

Arc Welding Outfit

This outfit will stay in the shop. Special shoes can be made to take with you, or take the hoof measurements and make up the shoe before going out.

Carbon Arc

The usefulness of a carbon arc depends on the electrical source available and the connections on the outfit.

The gas, arc, and carbon arc are discussed in Chapter VII and are mentioned here to complete the list of tools.

MISCELLANEOUS TOOLS

Halter and Nylon Rope

The strongest halter available, with a good nylon rope attached, is necessary. A catch rope is also needed as many horses are loose in the corral when you arrive. Try catching them in other ways first, using the rope only as a last resort. Some horses get so excited after they are roped that they will not stand.

Foot Ropes and Straps

Cotton sash cord of the heaviest weight available is best. It will not burn a horse readily, stays soft, and does not kink. There are three types of straps used: a twelve-inch strap with a "D" ring in each end; ankle straps with a buckle and "D" ring sewn in each; and a knee strap about two feet long with a buckle on the end and a ring in the center. Their use is covered in Chapter VI.

Hoof Tester

A hoof tester is a specially designed pair of tongs for locating tender areas in the foot. A tester may be purchased from a veterinarian supply house, but it doesn't take long to make one. Start with two pieces of round, five-eighths-inch iron twenty inches long. Put each round in a vise with about three-fourths of an inch sticking out. Heat this end and flatten. Chisel grooves across the flat face to give a better grip. Bend each side in the same shape and flatten the area where the two sections cross. Drill a hole in each section and put in a rivet. The distance between the jaws when closed should be at least seven inches so that they will fit over a large hoof. For a better grip and appearance, the ends of the handles can be shaped as shown in the illustration.

The use of this tester is covered in later chapters.

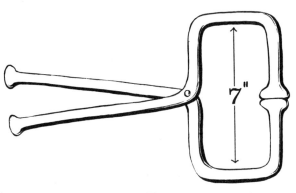

HOOF TESTER

Hoof Gauge

This instrument is used to measure the angle of the

hoof and the length of the toe from the point to the hair-line. I found that the branches on the one I purchased were too close together for the average horse, so I cut the gauge at the toe, spread the heels, and brazed it back together.

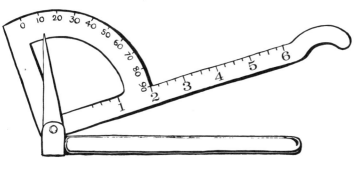

HOOF GAUGE

A hoof gauge can be made by welding a pointer at the toe of a plate shoe and attaching a hinged bar. The bar has a 90° bend at the point where it fits in the hinge, and a rounded bar is welded between the two sections. Using a protractor, mark each degree from 0°–90° on the rounded bar. Now mark the edge of the long, straight bar every one-fourth inch, with a larger mark for every inch. Use shims to tighten the bar in the hinge.

Burning Iron

Almost any small piece of iron can be used to burn the wall above a crack. Mine has a semicircular burning edge about one-sixteenth inch thick. A straight edge about a half-inch long would work just as well; but

the rounded edge gives a pleasing appearance, and I feel
it is my trademark. Burn only as deep as necessary, depending on the depth of the crack and the thickness
of the wall. This will be deeper at the toe than at the
quarter but rarely over three eighths of an inch. I carry
a small tank of bottled gas to heat the iron. The iron will
burn the hoof wall before it becomes red-hot.

Foot Stand

A stand is used to hold the horse's foot, and it takes
a lot of strain off of your back if you are shoeing all day.
Some horses are so used to a stand that they put all their
weight on it; consequently, the hoof cannot be held without the stand. It is better to do without a stand, if possible, as it is just one more tool to carry and is a safety
hazard if you or the horse should fall on it. Most stands
have three legs, are made of wood or iron, and are about
fourteen inches high.

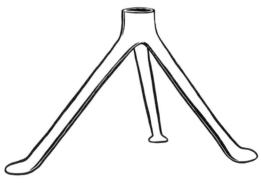

FOOT STAND

48

Portable Light

As the days get shorter in winter, a light is needed when working on a horse's hoof. A lamp, with clamps to attach to a car battery or with a regular plug and an extension cord, can be made.

The base of my lamp is a round cultivator disc with a five-foot pipe welded to the disc and a switch and flood lamp mounted on top. This device works very well as it can be moved wherever it is needed to put the best light on the hoof. Overhead lights, which cause shadows, are not satisfactory. Be sure to use heavy-duty bulbs as a regular bulb will probably burn out if the lamp is knocked down. Carry extra bulbs, at least a fifty-foot extension cord, and a plug to screw into a light bulb socket if there is no regular outlet available.

Shoeing Box

This is the box that holds the tools and nails. The box must have a handle or sit on casters so that it can be moved quickly out of the horse's way, if necessary. The sides should be open so that tools may be put in from either side. There must be some method used to keep the knife and rasp from coming in contact with other metal. Leather scabbards for each tool work well. Have compartments with lids for the nails so that, if the box is tipped, the nails will not be spilled and mixed together.

Horseshoe Storage

Some method must be devised for carrying a stock of shoes so that they will not become intermixed. This method should allow you to see at a glance which shoes must be restocked. A box with racks made from two-by-two's works well.

Miscellaneous Box

This box must be big enough to hold all the odds and ends that are seldom used but are still necessary—twitch, crescent wrench, fencing tool, foot ropes and ankle straps. Have a supply of one-quarter-inch rod for making extensions and calks and some pieces of one-eighth-inch iron for making clips.

This box should also contain basic veterinary supplies for immediate treatment of the feet, including iodine, sulfa powder, leather pads, pine tar, oakum (for packing under a pad), sheet metal (to make a plate that will slide in and out under the shoe for treating nail wounds, etc., without pulling the shoe), tin snips, leg linament, bandages (regular, elastic, and plaster of Paris), cotton, hoof dressings, fly spray, file, whetstone, felt, epoxy glue, and an assortment of nails to fit any shoe. A set of bell boots is also useful to put on the horse when experimenting with weight or different methods of shoeing.

This box can also be used to hold a book of bills, a pen, and a reference or record book, indicating horses shod, any irregularities, and date shod.

III.

The Horseshoer
and People

THE FARRIER'S OBLIGATION

THE FARRIER IS A PROFESSIONAL and, as such, he must deal with the horse owners. To build up a good business, he must remember that a job well done is his best advertisement; always do the best work possible on every horse. A dependable, courteous man will soon have a good business with steady customers. He must be willing to talk with people about their horses, give advice, and explain why he is doing something in a certain way.

The farrier is obligated to have good equipment and to keep it in shape. He must also have a complete supply of shoes available for every foreseeable situation.

The professional horseshoer should keep a record of horses shod, date shod, and any peculiarities. This record is a handy reference for later questions on a particular horse and is also useful for income tax purposes. A good farrier will generally guarantee his work for about six weeks, and a record of shoeing dates will prevent any confusion. The shoer cannot be expected to reset a shoe at no charge if the horse loses it when paw-

51

ing in the fence wire, or if the horse has such broken or dry feet that they cannot hold a shoe.

The farrier must present an itemized, dated statement to the horse owner for income tax purposes (see the following example).

BOB WISEMAN—SCIENTIFIC HORSESHOER

Phone 573-2400

P.O. Box 1103

Burns, Oregon

Name _____ Date _____

Labor: _____ Horses @_____/Hd_____

Shoes: _____ Size_____ Type _____ @ _____/Pr._____

Nails: _____ Horses@25c/Horse _____

Travel: _____

Corrective shoeing and/or special shoes: _____

Other: _____

_____

TOTAL _____

Never drop nail stubs or trash around the working area if you expect to be called back; put the stubs in the cuff of your pants.

Above all, keep studying, adopt sensible new ideas, and keep trying to improve your work. You owe it to the customers and their horses to learn all you can. If you please your customers and do a good job on their horses, you will have enough money to keep shoes on your children and even buy a side of bacon once in a while.

THE HORSE OWNER'S OBLIGATION

Now let us consider the horse owner. Above all, he should have the horse in before the farrier arrives. If the horse has faulty gaits, kicks, or is in any way unusual, the owner should tell the farrier. He should also state how the horse will be used and what type of shoes are preferred.

A level, clean, dry area should be provided, with no obstructions that could endanger the horse or shoer. Shade in summer and protection from the weather in the winter are of real help. Make sure the horse has clean, dry feet; this is a time-saver and convenience for the farrier. If the horse is being brought in out of the mud, have a sack handy to wipe his feet. It seems like the best cure for a constipated horse is to shoe him, so have a broom and shovel handy too.

If you have children, keep them quiet and out of the way.

Trimming the horse's feet in the fall and during the winter will make the farrier's job much easier in the spring. The hoof will also be in good condition for holding a shoe; it is much more difficult to keep a shoe on a broken hoof.

Handle the horse's feet while he is being groomed. Such attention will make subsequent shoeings easier for the horse and the shoer. If you don't handle the horse's feet yourself, allow the farrier a "free hand," even if you would rather have him hit you than your "baby." Remember that, if the horseshoer is competent, "Old Paint" will not only have new shoes but will be a better horse for it.

If you have been graining your horse heavily and he is excitable, cut down on his ration for a few days before he is shod and exercise him as much as possible.

Never have your horse shod unless he needs it. On the other hand, don't wait until he is so sore that he doesn't know which foot to limp on. If he needs shoes "all around," don't shoe the front hoofs only, on the assumption that where the front feet go, the hind feet will have to follow.

Don't wait until the last minute to call the farrier. If you know that you will be needing the horse, make an appointment ahead of time to be sure he gets shod. This is especially true just before fairs, roundups, horse shows, hunting season, etc.

It sometimes helps, if you are holding the horse, to stand on the same side that the farrier is working on so that the horse doesn't have to worry about people on both sides. Keep the horse's head up so that he is better balanced and will not put his weight on the shoer.

In fly season, spray the horse first. Don't try to thin his tail or do anything with him while the shoer is working.

Finally, be prepared to pay as soon as you receive the bill. If you don't, it won't be long before you are nailing the shoes on yourself or riding an unshod horse.

Shoeing Charges

What the farrier should charge depends on a number of factors. Going rates vary in different parts of the country, as well as from farrier to farrier in a given area. Thus I shall not attempt to set specific rates, but will discuss some of the factors that should be taken into consideration in deciding how much to charge.

First of all, the more skillful farrier with a complete stock of supplies and equipment can justifiably charge more than the ordinary horseshoer. To be taken into account also is the size of the horse (big feet take longer), how much he fights or kicks, and whether he has to be tied up or thrown down. The last item represents a penalty for owners who do not take time to work with their horse's feet. The charge may be more during the busy season, especially if an owner needs his horse shod *right now*. Corrective shoeing, winter shoeing with calks and pads, putting the first shoes on a colt, putting the first set of shoes on in the spring, and shoeing a stud in season all take longer and warrant an extra charge.

Customers who use your services regularly, always have their horses tied and ready for shoeing, pay their bills promptly, and in general are co-operative and fair deserve preferred treatment. Since they make work easier for you and are not credit risks, you can afford to charge them less. Give them as much of a bargain as you can.

Another factor is the distance you have to travel. If a number of horses are to be shod at one place, often you can absorb travel expense, but if you must go some distance to shoe one horse, you will almost certainly have to charge for mileage.

Horse owners find out, after using fly-by-night shoers, that a good farrier is cheap at his price. Most people realize that horseshoeing is hard work, there is some risk involved, and the farrier has a big investment in his

55

outfit; therefore, they don't mind paying a fair price.

When determining the charge, remember the Golden Rule. Also remember that blacksmiths go to hell for two reasons: pounding on cold iron and not charging enough.

IV.

The Horseshoer
and Horses

HORSE PSYCHOLOGY

As you gain experience, it will become easier to judge a horse's temperament. Understanding the horse is necessary in order to know how to treat him. Some horses will respond remarkably well to a good whack in the belly; but, on the other hand, you wouldn't want to do that to a high-strung horse that was just scared and trying to get away.

Horses can think; there is no doubt about it, but they cannot reason. To a horse there is only an effect and not a cause. Horses learn largely through repetition, but if you let them think about something for a while, they will learn faster. A horse doesn't learn very much when he gets too excited to think—all he wants to do is put distance between himself and whatever is scaring him. There's the old saying about stopping to think; a horse figures, "Why stop when I can do it on the run?"

The first thing to do is instill confidence in the horse and keep him from becoming excited. Talking calmly and moving slowly and steadily are very helpful. Such carefulness is especially important just before a storm or change in the weather when the horse is likely to be

57

keyed up and let his imagination overcome his good sense.

A horse's natural instinct is to be free, and he has a definite tendency to claustrophobia. To avoid this tendency, tie the horse where he can see around and as loosely as possible, while allowing you to get the job done. Watch his eyes, ears, and muscles; these will tell you what he is going to do before he does it. Tying another horse close by helps, but don't try to work in a spot where there are many horses or people moving about. Giving him a little grain before you start will show him that you mean no harm, but don't let him eat while he is being shod. No animal likes to be bothered while he is eating.

I always like to bend over in front of the horse and let him smell me and feel me with his nose before I start to work; a horse uses his nose in the same way we use our fingers. Be sure to leave a horse's nose alone, especially a colt's.

Never stare a horse straight in the eye or you are likely to scare him. If you want to move the horse, pick up the lead rope and walk off without looking at him. You may have to give a little tug so he understands that you want him to follow.

Now you are ready to start work. *Never reach down and grab a horse's leg suddenly.* Instead, slide your hand down his leg. I generally touch him with my shoulder before touching the leg; this also will put you in a safer position if he should jump or rear.

Remember that horses are one-sided. This means that just because they learn something on one side does not mean they know it on the other. This point cannot be overstressed. A horse may also be very gentle when three of his legs are handled but kick like a mule with the fourth one. Always respect the horse you are working on. Not every horse has good "horse sense." Quite a few sober-looking ponies have peculiar ideas and superstitions that they must eat with the grass.

Before knowing how to handle an individual horse (horses are all individuals), the reason he acts as he does must be discovered. There are three problem types to consider: 1. the horse whose feet have never been handled (he doesn't know what is wanted), 2. the horse that is just plain scared, and 3. the horse that is spoiled (this is the worst horse to work on as he will kick if he thinks he can get away with it). Patience is the answer to types 1 and 2. Take your time with these horses, and the next time they will not be so hard to shoe. Number 3 is a completely different problem, and if a good whack or two doesn't straighten him up, it is best to tie a leg up or lay him down, often to the consternation of the person who did the spoiling.

Horseshoers are expendable. If one of these "wall-eyed pets" kicks you, you won't get much sympathy from the owner. After all, isn't that part of the horseshoer's job? The owner would never dream of handling the horse's feet himself—he doesn't want to get kicked. Well, neither does the horseshoer. It's not the farrier's job to teach the horse manners but to tack on the shoes; so, for success without broken bones, tie him down. It is amazing how much conceit this will take out of him, and nobody gets hurt, not even the shoer.

A really successful farrier keeps his self-control at all times and avoids showing even the slightest bit of temper, even when he is hurt. (Forget your troubles and think of the horse's problems.) Self-control and patience are the real keys to handling horses; try to establish a basis for confidence between yourself and the horse.

Some horses can be bluffed by growling at them a little, but it has to be done at the right time. Remember that the horse will be used for many years and cannot learn all he needs to know about shoeing in one easy lesson. Proper treatment will get a colt off to a good start, and he will learn to trust men. Such a horse is easy to catch and will do a fair day's work in exchange for fair treatment.

Reward and Punishment

Humiliation many times is much better than pain and is the most efficient way of punishing a horse, especially a spoiled one. Throwing him down and holding him there is the best way to show him the error of his ways. *Never* hit a horse below the knee.

Reward the horse when he is good and punish him when he is bad. Make this treatment in line with the circumstances, and the horse will be easier to shoe each time.

BAD HABITS DURING SHOEING

Some horses figure that shoeing is something they cannot avoid but give them credit for trying all kinds of ways to get out of it. In this section most of their methods and possible countermeasures are discussed.

60

Biting

It is usually obvious if the horse is thinking of biting, and generally a low growl will change his mind. Remember that horses use their noses for investigation, and this one may simply be finding out more about you with no intention of biting. If this is true, let him satisfy his curiosity. If you duck when hearing the horse's mouth open, he will miss you; however, if he bites or tries to bite, a slap on the mouth will probably cure him. Don't slap the horse if he is scared and trying to protect himself; just keep out of his way. Wear a hat or cap when working on a spoiled horse that may bite. Put a wire nose-basket on him, cross-tie him, or have someone hold him and keep him from biting.

Sulking

Few horses will sulk, but if one does, divert his attention. A sudden movement that he doesn't expect will do this. A good method is to suddenly grab and pinch the upper foreleg.

Leaning on You

Some horses will put a lot of weight on you and others practically none. Both kinds are difficult to shoe. Some horses will purposely throw their weight on you or expect you to hold them up; there is no excuse for this unless the horse has always been shod on a stand. Never let him lean on you; let him fall instead. Sometimes moving the leg to a different position or farther ahead will help. If the horse is a real problem, tie the front or hind leg up and lead him around until he learns to maintain his bal-

61

ance. He may have to be tied up on each side; remember that a horse is "one-sided."

Constant Movement

Some horses just cannot stand still. These are high-strung horses or horses that are worrying about something. Have as much patience with them as you can and try to remove the cause of their nervousness. Try to work in a place with which they are familiar. It may help to tie one of their companions close by or remove a tempting sack of oats, etc. Try not to get them excited, especially when catching them and first starting to work. A few extra minutes spent at this point will save time in the long run.

Kicking and Striking

There are two reasons for kicking and striking. One is that the horse is afraid and trying to protect himself; kicking is the horse's natural method of defense. The other is that he is spoiled. If the horse is spoiled and his owner will not allow him to be punished or his leg tied up, it would be better to leave quietly rather than get kicked. Use good judgment with these horses, remembering that extra time spent here will make future shoeings easier, especially when you are dealing with a colt.

If the horse strikes or rears, tie him shorter and lower than usual so that he cannot get his feet above you.

Some of these habits may be very aggravating. Be patient, however, and maintain self-control while trying to outsmart the horse without making the job harder for yourself. The horse is a gullible creature and is bluffed easily. Once you start something, always finish it. Impress him that disobedience brings punishment and obedience brings reward. Remember that each horse is an individual and must be analyzed so that he is not angered or antagonized unintentionally.

V.

Shoeing

Removing Shoes and Trimming

The first step when pulling the shoe is to cut or straighten the clinches. Use a heavy hammer and a clinch cutter (buffer). Bring the foot forward and hold it on your knee while cutting the clinches. If you have a regular buffer, you may prefer to hold the foot between your legs. A cold chisel, file, or hacksaw can be used in emergencies.

When the clinches are cut, put the foot into working position and insert the pull-off tongs under one of the shoe branches. Pry up each side until the shoe is loose and then twist the shoe, thereby pulling the toe nails and removing the shoe. When prying on the sole, do not use too much pressure as the sensitive tissues under the sole can be crushed. If there are any nails or stubs left in the wall, remove them so that they will not dull the hoof nipper or cause a new nail to deflect and prick the horse.

If you are not going to reset the shoes right away, drive out the nail stubs and fasten the shoes together in pairs for storage. When shoeing several horses, it is a a good idea to tag each set of shoes with the horse's name.

If the feet are sore for any reason or have very poor horn, pull only one shoe, trim the hoof, and nail on a new shoe before pulling the others. Always examine the wear of the old shoe. If the foot is balanced correctly and the horse is using the leg normally, the shoe will be evenly worn. Excessive wear at the toe or heels may indicate that pain is causing the horse to walk on the toe or heels or that something is affecting the stride. A short stride wears the toe (except in founder—see Chapter IX), and a long stride wears the heels.

When observing the shoe, if one side of the *toe* is badly worn, it indicates that the foot is breaking over at this point instead of at the center of the toe. If one *side* is worn more than the other, it indicates that the wall on this side is too high or that the shoe is fitted too fine (too close to the center of the hoof, so that it bears more weight than it should). If one of the *heels* is worn more than the other, it indicates that this heel is higher, or, if the foot toes in, the outside heel will wear. In order to counteract the increased wear on the outside heel, for example, lower the wall around the inside toe and vice versa.

Stand the horse on a level surface and check the feet from the front and side. A crooked foot shows up readily from the front. Check the angle of the foot from the side so that it can be made identical to that of the pastern. Check the heels of the front and back feet to see that each pair is of the same height. Watch the feet in action; a foot that looks all right on the ground may not fly straight in motion. Improper foot action may be caused by a problem in the pastern or leg and involve a corrective shoe, in addition to trimming, in many cases.

After checking the old shoe, the angle of hoof alignment, and the hoof's path in flight, you will have a good idea what needs to be done. Sight across the heels after

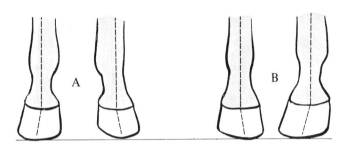

FAULTS OF TRIMMING

Feet broken in—To correct, lower the outside wall.

Feet broken out—To correct, lower the inside wall.

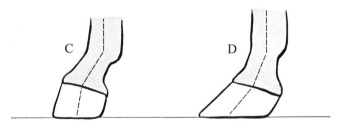

Foot angle broken forward— To correct, lower the heels.

Foot angle broken back— To correct, lower the toe.

Note: These illustrations of hoof angles are not normal and are caused by incorrect trimming.

cleaning the hoof; the high side will generally be apparent. This procedure should verify your observation from the front. With your knife, trim the sole around the wall down to live horn; this will indicate the height of the wall.

When trimming a crooked hoof, start on the low heel and work around to the high side, cutting deeper as you go. If you start on the high side, you might be cutting too deeply when you get to the other side, which is already low.

If the horse is not going to be shod or will be subjected to a considerable amount of concussion on a hard surface, leave the wall a little longer than usual. Remember that the sole is lower at the quarters, making the wall look higher. *Be extremely careful not to cut the wall too low at the quarters.* Cut the bars to the same depth as the rest of the wall so that they will support their share of the shoe. Taper the points a little so they won't catch on rocks and tear.

Leave the frog alone in a normal foot. The good Lord put it there for a reason (see Chapter I on "Hoof Functions"), and it is the key to a healthy hoof. In the past a common practice has been to trim the frog and "open" the heels. If the frog is trimmed, the hoof does not expand properly and contracted heels will eventually result.

Lower the sole only enough so that the shoe does not put pressure on it; however, a little pressure in the toe area is permissible. Cutting out the sole lets the foot dry out and leaves the sensitive tissues more subject to injury. Trim off the old flakes if they are building up around the frog and preventing it from functioning properly.

If the hoof is very crooked, as often happens in cow-hocked horses, for instance (see Chapter X and the illustration, "Conformation Defects II"), you may not want to trim the low side (inside, in this case) at all, but simply rasp it level for the shoe and lower the high side as much as possible. This type of foot may need leather shims or a thickened branch under the low side in addition to trimming.

Hold the nippers in such a way that the wall will be cut evenly and will not taper from the inside out. The depth of the first cut at the heel will depend on the desired angle. If the horse has a long toe, it may not be necessary to trim the heels at all; simply rasp them level for the shoe, and vice versa. If the front feet, for example, are not the same size, prepare the larger foot first, making it as small as possible.

A simple rule to remember is *lower the side that points*; in other words, if the toe points out, lower the outside wall from toe to heel. There are few exceptions to this rule. Also rasp the outside wall as much as possible. Using the white line for a guide, leave enough wall to hold the shoe and support the weight.

In order to change the position of the horse's legs to help correct defects of conformation, change the angle of the hoof. In other words, to move the horse's legs back, lower the toe; to move the legs forward, lower the heels.

When balancing and leveling, let the foot hang naturally and sight across the heels. See that the heels are the same height and that there are no high or low areas along the bottom of the wall. If the wall around the inside of the toe is high, the outside heel also may appear high, and vice versa; therefore, be careful where you rasp until you are sure that it is producing the desired effect.

In addition to balancing the foot so that it is straight and the angle is correct, the wall must also be leveled so that a flat shoe will be solid and will not rock.

If the horse is to remain unshod, leave one-quarter-inch more horn than normal for shoeing, and bevel the outer edge of the wall about half of its width with the rasp so that the wall will not break out. This is especially important if the horse has been shod for a long time, as the fibers of the wall become less elastic and will break out easily.

It is a good idea to let the horse go unshod for at least two or three months of the year. When a horse is first turned out after having been stabled for some time, it is best to leave the shoes on him for a few days, since, if the hoofs are not trimmed closely after the shoes are pulled, the horse's playfulness could cause a foot to break out. A close trim will also keep snow from balling up in the hoof if the horse is turned out in the winter.

PREPARING THE FEET

Preparation of the feet may involve more than the actual trimming. If possible, dry feet should be soaked prior to shoeing. This may take a week or more, depending on how dry the feet are, the method used, and time spent in applying moisture (see "Hoof Care" in Chapter I). If there are cracks, they will have to be treated before a shoe is applied. If the crack is complete, it will have to be immobilized by one of the methods described in Chapter IX. Once the crack is taken care of, a shoe applied correctly will protect it and allow healing to take place. If thrush or other diseases are present, the foot should be cleaned and treated before a shoe is applied.

SHOE SIZES

Unless a handmade shoe is used, the shoe size must be determined. The shoe must support the entire wall, but don't put any more "iron" under the horse than is needed. The hind feet will usually take a size smaller than the front feet because they are smaller and not as rounded.

The main things to consider in determining shoe sizes are the nail holes and the length of the heels. On a front foot, the last hole should not be behind the widest part of the foot. In other words, the holes should generally be in the front half of the shoe (see illustration, "Normal Shoe," in Chapter VIII). For a hind foot the last nail may be a little farther back. The amount of expansion desired will govern the placing of the last nail in both cases. Make sure that the branches are long enough to support the entire wall, but do not project too far beyond the heel. This varies according to the work the horse will do and the angle of the hoof. For horses doing fast work, such as cutting horses, do not let the branch extend beyond the heels. For horses with a long, sloping foot, longer branches will help to support the rear tendons and protect the overhanging heels.

The way the foot is trimmed will make a difference in the amount of iron needed. If the heels are lowered and the toe left long, a larger shoe will be needed than if the foot is shortened. Also, if the shoe is fit full and rounded at the toe, it will need more iron.

GENERAL RELATION OF WEIGHT TO SHOE SIZE

Weight of Mature Horses	*Shoe Sizes*
400 pounds	Pony-shoes
600 "	00
800 "	0
1,000 "	1
1,300 "	2
1,500 "	3

A horse's feet will change size as the moisture content varies. This means that a shoe that was right for the horse in the fall may be too small in the spring. Also, if a colt's shoes are saved for him over the winter, they will be too small in the spring. I might add that if a colt's shoes are hard-surfaced, he will often outgrow them before he outwears them.

The hot shoe blanks with unfinished heels allow more leeway in trimming the heels to size than keg shoes with finished heels (see "Hot and Cold Shoeing Methods" later in this chapter).

FITTING THE SHOE

Fit the shoe to the hoof and not the hoof to the shoe.

71

This is good advice, but most people really don't know what it means. In this statement, "hoof" means the hoof as indicated by the white line and not the outer border of the wall. When the hoof has undergone changes because of faulty shoeing or conformation, the shoe should be shaped as nearly as possible to the shape that the normal hoof had before the change occurred. The coffin bone gives the hoof its shape, and since the white line corresponds to the shape of the coffin bone, it is the true shape. Fitting the shoe so that the nail holes lie as nearly as possible over the white line is very important. Nails started into the outer edge of the white line do the least damage to the wall and hold the shoe securely.

Since the wall is thicker at the toe than at the heels and since keg shoes do not have the nail holes set in much farther at the toe than at the heels to compensate for this added thickness, driving all the nails in the white line will result in the wall overhanging the shoe at the toe. Lack of this compensation is a bad feature of American-made shoes as the toe must then be rasped off to fit the shoe. This is particularly true of front feet because the wall of the hind feet normally does not vary so much from toe to heel. Usually the shoe can be set a little farther forward; however, the toe nails will then be driven into the wall. If the hoof is normal and perfectly leveled and a level shoe is nailed on, the toe nails may be left out completely. Nails driven into the wall do not have much holding power and make unnecessary holes in the horn.

Practice making each shoe perfectly level. When the iron is twisted, it may be necessary to hit it on the edge to level the shoe. To check, lay the shoe on a flat surface and see if it will rock.

When fitting the shoe, remember that the horse has a left and a right foot. The outside branch will generally be fuller than the inside branch. Hind shoes are bent in a completely different way from front shoes. A front shoe has a rounded toe; a hind shoe has a pointed toe. If a hind shoe is made too round at the toe, the hoof must be trimmed to make it fit the shoe. To fit the shoe at the toe, it is usually necessary to close the shoe slightly first. Now lay it across the heel of the anvil and straighten each branch, from the toe back, about halfway to the heels. This points the toe but leaves the shoe wide at the quarters. Now bend the heels to make a good fit. The foot has less expanse when it is off of the ground, so don't fit the shoe too finely in the heels or the wall will spread over the shoe and not receive the necessary support.

Many horses have one heel that is longer than the other. If this is the case, make one branch longer. To do this, place the shoe over the anvil horn with the toe away from you and the branch that will be shorter on top. Pound the shoe, starting a couple of inches back from the toe, bringing the iron around to lengthen the other side. If the horse has normal feet (opposite pairs alike), bend a front and hind shoe to the correct shape and try them on as you trim the feet. Make any necessary adjustments and use these shoes as rough patterns for the opposite feet.

Making and fitting a handmade shoe is covered in Chapter VIII.

Nails and Nailing

Various sizes and types of nails are available. There is a one-quarter-inch difference in length between the sizes. You will use more No. 5 nails than any other size as they fit most shoes that correspond to a No. 0 or No. 1. For smaller shoes, a No. 4 nail may be right, and a No. 6 nail will hold a No. 2 shoe. The nail must fit the hole. Pick a nail that goes through the hole about three-fourths its length, and when driven, it will be immovable in the hole. The nailhead should project slightly above the shoe when seated. If the nail does not fit, use a different size or enlarge the hole slightly.

Use small nails in poor-quality horn and never drive nails through or near cracks. If the wall is broken out, open the nail hole a little and use a larger nail so that it will reach above the break and get a grip in the sound horn. Never drive a crooked nail, as the bend in it may put pressure on the sensitive quick. If a nail does not feel or sound right, pull it out and start over. Occasionally a nail will bend around or even bend back on itself. It may have hit the stub of an old nail, or fibers of the foot may turn it; and, in either case, it would be dangerous to drive it on in.

The tapered side of the head is roughened. This helps the farrier since he does not have to look at each nail to see which way to drive it, and it also helps hold the nail tightly in the hole. The flat side of the nailhead always goes out. The flat side of the point should be started against the outside of the hole unless the shoe is not centered and must move across the foot slightly. In this case, place the beveled edge of the nail against the inner side of the hole on the branch opposite the direction that you want the shoe to move. As the head is seated in the hole, the bevel moves the shoe slightly.

The beveled point is not effective unless the nail is driven forcefully. This permits the expert farrier to adjust the height that the nail will be driven as he drives it. If the nail is to go higher, he uses light taps. The expert can also tell, by the sound and feel, when the nail emerges, and will rarely prick a horse.

If the horse is pricked, the nail should be pulled, the hole opened, and iodine poured into the opening. A nail should not be put in this hole, and the owner should be notified so that he may give the horse a tetanus shot or at least watch for any adverse effects. If pus should form, soak the bottom of the hoof in Epsom salts. It is best to call a veterinarian in cases such as this.

Put nails in your pants cuff as they are handy there; and if the horse jumps around, you will have your nails with you wherever you end up.

Before putting the shoe on the foot, make a mental picture of the white line and the thickness of the wall. In this way you will know exactly where to put the shoe, and if it moves, you can start over without pricking the horse accidentally.

There is a difference of opinion about which nails should be driven first. The main objective is to get two nails into the shoe as quickly as possible so that, if the horse jerks away, he will not throw the shoe. Some farriers drive a nail in each side, or the rear nails first to hold the shoe in place. I prefer to drive one of the front nails first, unless these holes do not lie directly over the white line. This allows you to pivot the shoe slightly if it is not exactly where you want it and then drive a side nail to hold the shoe in place.

If the shoe moves back slightly after the first nail is driven, the nail was started on the outside of the white line. Taking the path of least resistance, the nail has slipped back into the white line, moving the shoe with it. *Drive the first nail in a hole that lies directly over the white line.*

Keep your nails in the front half of a front foot and in the front two-thirds of a hind foot. Expansion is more important in the front feet, as they are flatter and also carry more of the horse's and rider's weight. In a wide hoof, the nails may be driven farther back since there is little danger of binding the foot.

In an ordinary foot, six nails are enough, leaving the toe nails out. If seven nails are used, the seventh one should go on the outside where the wall is longer and slightly thicker.

The nails should be driven to a uniform height in a sound foot. They should be aimed toward the rear of the hoof when they are started so that they are driven somewhat parallel to the horn fibers, not at a 90-degree angle to the shoe. A nail driven parallel to the fibers cuts less of them, and as the nail is seated in the hole, it is bent back, forming a clinch where it comes out of the shoe. This helps to tighten and lock the nails. Aim the toe nails more toward the rear of the hoof than the heel nails, which may be straight up and down.

The holes in a well-made shoe are slanted so that the

nail may be driven at the same angle as the wall. This inward slant is graduated from the toe to the heel so that the last heel nail will be almost straight, conforming to the angle of the wall. The inside wall is straighter than the outside wall. With a little practice, you will learn to feel the slant of the wall and aim the nails so that they all come out about three-fourths of an inch above the shoe. A nail driven low destroys the least possible horn (holes in the horn never close up), has its full width forming the clinch, and has a stronger hold on the wall than a nail driven higher because it is pulling more at a right angle.

After the nails are all driven, they are drawn up, or seated, by holding a piece of iron or the jaw of the nippers against the end of the nail, where it comes out of the horn, as the head is tapped. Tighten nails alternately on either side to keep the strain on the shoe even.

When nailing a pad under a shoe, fit the shoe first. Then nail the pad to the shoe with two side nails. Cut the nail ends even with the pad, trim the pad to fit the shoe, and nail the shoe to the foot. Pull the stubs that held the pad and finish nailing the shoe to the foot.

If you are going to reset used shoes, be sure to check the nail holes, as they may be worn. If the holes are too large, the best way to tighten them is to throw the shoe away. The holes can be welded shut and repunched or a larger nail can be used, but you should remember that a larger nail ruins more horn. Another method is to put the branch over the horn of the anvil and hammer on the outside edge hard enough to narrow the hole slightly.

Finishing Off

The last step is called "finishing." The foot is taken forward, and the nails are nipped off, leaving only a slight protrusion to be used to form the clinch. The nails on the side toward you should be cut first so that, if the horse jerks his foot, you will not be cut. Cut the nails so that the clinch will be an eighth of an inch long when bent over. The heel nails should be cut slightly longer than the toe nails as the wall is straighter at the heels and the clinch has to be bent farther. The strength of the clinch is in the bend, and leaving a long clinch does not make it any stronger. It is also possible for a long clinch to get straightened out and cut the opposite leg. Now use the clincher to bend the nail end down. If the clincher does not contact the nail end, bend it out slightly so that the clincher will grab it. Use the pull-off tongs for this, with one edge against the bottom of the shoe and the other behind the nail. Now use hammer to smooth the clinch and seat it into the wall slightly. Be careful not to pull the clinch down through the wall with the clincher or tongs; this is easy to do in soft horn. If you don't have a clincher, place something solid against the nailhead and use your driving hammer to bend the nail over and form the clinch.

In the final step, touch up the clinches and the lower edge of the wall with the file side of the rasp. For a very particular job, use the corner of the rasp to clean the area between the hoof and the shoe. This cleaned area is called a "voyaging groove."

Remember never to drop nail ends unless you are

working on a concrete floor where they can be swept up. They are real troublemakers and can end up in a horse's foot, in a tire, or even in a cow's stomach.

HOT AND COLD SHOEING METHODS

Much has been written on hot and cold shoeing methods, and the difference between the two methods seems to be a main point of controversy among horse people. Both methods have their advantages, and to be competent, a farrier must be able to do either. My personal opinion is that a cold shoe put on right is fine for the normal horse.

In order to clarify the two methods, I would define cold shoeing as fitting ready-made keg shoes to the hoof without heating them. This method also includes modifications to the shoe accomplished by welding. Heat is used in hot shoeing to make a shoe from a piece of iron or, much more common today, to fit and cut an unfinished blank to size.

Cold shoes may be purchased in various types and sizes. The advantages in cold shoeing are ease, mobility, and over-all low cost. Cold shoeing is especially convenient for the do-it-yourself horse owner as the materials needed are few and hence the investment is smaller.

I said cold shoeing was fine for the *normal* horse, but what about the others? There are many cases where you will need heat to get the job done. With a forge, welder, and accessory tools, possibilities are unlimited, and you can handle any case that comes up. You can take pride in your accomplishments and look forward to each new challenge. This is something the cold-shoe man never knows. Also the farrier who operates this way commands a higher price because of his skill and versatility.

One thing an unscrupulous man can do with a hot shoe is to burn the wall in order to seat the shoe instead of taking the time to rasp the wall perfectly flat and nail a flat shoe to it. This is a bad practice if overdone as it tends to draw moisture out of the hoof. This is exactly what you don't want. A red-hot shoe applied for an instant does less damage than a shoe at a cooler heat that is left on long enough for the heat to conduct into the sensitive tissues. A hot shoe will mark the nail holes, making it easy to see that they are all on the white line.

Aside from making special shoes, there are other advantages to hot shoeing—a perfect fit on odd-shaped hoofs can be made, a certain amount of hardening and tempering can be done, and nail holes can be punched where needed and slanted correctly for the individual hoof. Shoes can also be modified with clips, lateral extensions, and trailers, and the foot surface can be seated out so that the sole doesn't put pressure against it. Hard-surfaced shoes can be bent without cracking them, and work-horse shoes that are too large to be bent when cold can be fitted easily. Since the shoe can be cut to size and modified, a much smaller inventory is needed.

For speed and efficiency you will need to develop a hot-shoeing system. Have a stout ring to which the horse can be tied so he will be handy to the forge. The ring should be about level with the withers so the horse isn't likely to get his front feet over the rope. Always tie the rope with a slip knot.

After observing the conformation and gaits, if necessary, use the trimming tools and prepare all four feet. Take four shoe blanks with you (you can stick them in your boot top), and as each hoof is trimmed, mark a shoe so that you will know where to bend it. Use chalk or soapstone for marking and develop a code, such as an inward line to indicate bending in and an outward line to indicate bending out. Dent the shoes with a hammer or tongs, or use a file, so you can tell the difference between left and right, front and hind shoes. Mark the outside of front and the inside of hind shoes, or use your own code. Lay all four shoes on top of each other in the fire. Then, as you work on the bottom one, the second one will be hot, etc. When the shoe is about right, use a pritchel to carry it to the hoof and apply it for a second to check fit and length of heels. Reheat the shoe, trim the heels, pritchel the holes if needed, and level up the shoe. Then cool it and nail it to the hoof.

LOST SHOES

Shoes are lost for many reasons, but the better the foot, the better it will hold a shoe. It is hard to keep shoes on horses with dry, shelly, broken-out, thin-walled, or flat feet. Horses with bad habits, such as pawing in fences, will lose their shoes in the wire, etc. It takes more skill to keep shoes on a fast-working horse than on one kept at slower gaits.

A horseshoer's motto should be, "If it isn't right, it won't stay on." Some of the more common faults include not starting the nail against the outside of the hole, using nails of the wrong size, and driving the nails too low, too close together, or so high that only the tip of the nail can be clinched.

The nails should be *in the white line* and should be driven in the direction of the hoof fibers. The nail holes should be pritcheled in the same direction that the nail is driven and not opened too wide. Nail holes that are too small will let the head of the nail wear off completely; whereas holes that are too large will let the nailhead slip through after only a small amount of wear.

If the heels are kept tight, the shoe will stay on. Using a shoe that is too small will put the heel nails too far forward to hold the heels tightly. A common error is leaving the heels too long on the front shoes so that they are pulled off by the hind shoes.

Many shoes are lost because the foot is not balanced correctly, the wall is not made perfectly level, or the shoe is not perfectly flat. If you can rock the shoe before you start nailing, it will flatten somewhat as it is nailed down, but this puts a strain on the nails and may cause them to pull out or break. Nails should be clinched alternately from one side to the other so that there is no extra strain on the nails of one side.

There are many things the horse owner can do in addition to making certain that the horse is properly shod. The horse should not be worked a great deal on a hard surface. This causes concussion, which weakens the nails and is harmful to the horse.

Leaving the shoes on too long, working a tired horse, and lunging a horse in snow, mud, or sand can all cause shoe loss. In addition, changing a horse from extremely wet to dry surroundings, or vice versa, will cause the foot to change size and the shoe to loosen.

Remember that nail holes may wear out before shoes. This happens if the shoe is left on after it becomes loose. If you want the shoer to reset these shoes, don't expect them to stay on too long. The heel holes wear first because of expansion. A larger nail can be used in these holes; however, it makes a larger hole in the horn. The holes can also be closed slightly by a blow on the outside edge of the branch.

Above all, lost shoes can easily be avoided by the farrier's good horseshoeing techniques and the owner's periodic checks on hoofs and shoes. A competent farrier is well worth his price to the conscientious horse owner.

VI

Handling Rough Horses

SOME FARRIERS enjoy handling rough horses and take pride in never starting on a horse that they don't finish. With the proper equipment and know-how, this work can be relatively safe and will command a premium, as many horseshoers will not work on such horses. Is your insurance paid up?

You can often tell when you are going to have a rough horse to shoe; people will come from all directions to watch the fun. There is always a certain amount of excitement involved when a two-hundred-pound man matches his skill against a muscular "hay muncher" weighing half a ton or more. Superior intelligence and ropes more than equalize this disadvantage, but if you are afraid of him, keep it under your hat.

First of all, be careful which horses you put in this class. Certainly a colt who doesn't know any better or is scared cannot be considered a rough horse. Once this type of horse knows what is wanted and realizes that he is not being hurt, he will be easy to shoe. The horses considered here are generally the older, spoiled horses that were not handled properly when first shod. It would take more time to train these horses to stand still while being shod than they are worth; therefore, special methods have been devised for working with them, depending upon how difficult they are to handle.

BLINDS

A blind can be very useful, and there is always a jacket, shirt, or sack available to tie over the horse's eyes. Never grab him suddenly after the blind is on, and talk reassuringly so that he knows where you are and is not surprised when you touch him. This simple method is all that is needed in many cases to get the job done without much trouble.

In other cases, a work bridle with blinkers may have a quieting effect, especially for the horses that are used to them.

THROWING

Here again, many methods can be used according to the circumstances involved. When shoeing horses, this is generally a last resort as it takes longer and is harder to do a good job on a horse in this position. It is a useful method for a spoiled horse because it will take a tremendous amount of conceit out of him. Always be sure to pick a soft area with no obstructions.

If it is necessary to shoe a number of wild horses that are not halterbroken and no chute is available, you can lasso the front legs, throwing the horse to the ground. Then have someone sit astride the horse's neck, pulling his nose up between his legs. Tie the legs while the horse is held in this position. Some men tie the horse's front

85

feet to a tree and the hind feet to a tractor, "stretching him out." In my opinion, this is a good example of what *not* to do. Practically all horses that need to be shod can be handled in some other way.

The best way to throw a horse is to tie a rope around the base of his neck with a bowline. Then lay the free end out and make him step over it with a hind foot. Quickly pull up the slack, and the rope will be under his fetlock. Pull the foot up and tie it to the neck rope. Go to the other side and tie another rope to the neck rope. Run this around the pastern of the foot still on the ground and up through the neck rope. If you are working alone, untie the horse's head at this time so that he will be free to fall. Pull the foot that is still on the ground up as far as possible, making him sit down, and tie the rope end to the neck rope with a slip knot. Make the horse lie down by pulling his nose back toward his withers. Now tie a front foot and a rear foot on the same side together by crossing the pastern of one leg over the cannon bone of the other; thus, the feet will be well separated and easier to shoe. I carry two ropes about seven feet long with a running loop in one end to tie the legs together. Roll him over and tie the other legs in the same way, then remove the ropes used to throw him. If you have a helper, it is a good idea to have him sit on the horse's neck so the horse doesn't hurt his head. Now wedge a tight bale of hay between the horse's legs so they are up where they can be worked on, or place a pole across his body and under his legs, getting someone to sit on the other end for leverage. A horse is less likely to injure himself or anyone else if his hind legs are secured before he goes down. If there is a better way of throwing a horse than this, "I'm from Missouri."

A small horse may be thrown by tying up his left front leg, bringing the halter rope over the back of his neck from the opposite side, and pulling his head up and back quickly, with enough force to throw him. The problem will then be holding him down and securing his hind feet. This could be dangerous. In the method described earlier, his hind feet are both already secured.

DRUGS

Many drugs are available to tranquilize or knock out a horse. They are useful in certain cases, but they can't always be depended upon to produce the desired effect. In addition, there is a fairly high mortality rate. Any time the physiological functions of an animal are so drastically altered as to immobilize it within minutes, a tremendous amount of stress is created within the animal's body. As a result, the animal may suffer a fatal shock; this is especially true of old or weak animals. If the horse should stop breathing, jump up and down on his rib cage.

Some of the drugs which are used successfully are nicotine, for intramuscular injection, and a powdered tranquilizer, which is mixed with feed and takes effect in about half an hour.

I have a gun-syringe projector in my outfit for emergency cases; however, I have never had to use it. It gives me self-confidence, as I know that no matter what kind of "man-killer" I may be hired to shoe, I will not have to leave without tacking a set of shoes on him.

87

Foot Hooks and Crooks

Some shoers use a foot crook shaped like a shepherd's staff to pull the hind leg forward. In my opinion, its use will never make the horse's legs easier to handle, and the horse is more likely to kick at a hard crook than at a hand.

At times, however, a foot hook will really save a lot of trouble. It is an iron rod about two feet long with a ring on one end, used as a handle, and a dull hook on the other end, which is about an inch across. Slip the hook behind the heel, pull the foot forward, and grasp only the hoof to take it back to a working position. It is hard to believe the effect this has on the horse if he is touchy about his legs. This method does not make the horse's legs much easier to handle, but, on the other hand, the shoer is getting paid to tack on the shoes, not train the horse.

Foot Hook

Hobbles

It is rarely desirable to hobble a horse when shoeing him as you cannot work on the hobbled feet. Occasionally, hobbling the front feet will enable you to work on the hind feet with no trouble, or hobbling a front and hind foot on the same side (sidelining) will enable you to work on the other side with little trouble. Hobbles work better when used with a blind since the horse is not as likely to go down. An area free of obstacles should always be chosen so that he will not break any ribs if he does go down.

Never leave hobbles on longer than necessary because they injure and inflame the tissues and bones. Many horses have been ruined in this way.

Running "W"

There are many variations of the running "W," but they all serve the same purpose, to jerk the horse's front feet out from under him. A horse may be thrown in this way by pulling him to his knees and then pulling his head back until he falls. In my opinion, it is safer and easier to pull his hind feet up when throwing him so that they are secured and not flying around (see "Throwing" earlier in this chapter).

A special surcingle, or belt, may be made, with rings on each side and one under the horse's belly, or a saddle may be used, with the stirrups acting as rings. Ankle straps with "D" rings in them should be placed on the horse's pasterns. A full running "W" is fastened to one side of the horse, down to the hoof, up to the stomach ring, down to the other hoof, and up through the ring on the other side. The rope is then pulled, bringing the horse to his knees. An incomplete "W" is fastened to the opposite foot instead of the side ring.

Stocks

In my opinion, there is just one use for shoeing stocks

—when horses or mules must be shod in "mass production" without regard for the individual animal or for trying to teach him anything. In all other cases, it is better to try to gentle the horse around his feet so he can be shod standing. This training pays off when your horse throws a shoe on top of a mountain somewhere, with no chance of getting home without a new one and a blizzard coming on.

Sometimes in this mass-production shoeing an electric grinder or hoof sander is used to level the hoof. This instrument is acceptable if care is taken not to lower the frog.

There are several kinds of stocks available, each using some method of squeezing or strapping the animal, and they are padded to minimize injuries. When the animal is secured, the better stocks can be turned on their side so that the feet are in a workable position. Part of the advantage of having the animal secured in this manner is lost in the process of strapping him in, as well as in the awkward position of trying to balance a foot while looking at it from the side. Although the latter problem is present in all throwing methods, it is especially troublesome when using stocks.

TWITCHES

A twitch is a useful device and can generally be made from material on hand. A good one can be made from a six-inch piece of broom handle with a hole drilled near one end. Put twine or chain through this hole so that it makes a loop about six inches in diameter. Put your hand through the loop, pull out the horse's upper lip, slide the twitch on the lip with the other hand, and twist the loop tight. If you are working by yourself, use a horse-shoe to twist the twine and then slip one branch through the side ring in the halter to hold it. The twitch will not give the same results on all horses, but at times it is all that is needed to make the shoeing job easier.

The twitch can also be put on the ear, and it usually has more effect in this area than putting it on the nose. Horses certainly don't want to lose an ear; seems they're partial to having two. It does, however, tend to make the horse head-shy and hard to bridle. Do not keep the twitch on indefinitely, but take it off after a while to see if he will stand still. Never use steady pressure, just punish the horse when he starts to act up.

Tying Up A Front Foot

Of the many methods for doing this, the simplest one is to carry a leather strap about two and a half feet long with a buckle in one end and a ring in the middle. Use this strap twisted in the shape of a figure 8 to fasten the horse's lower leg to his upper leg. This method holds the hoof in a good working position. Tying the leg in this fashion is an excellent method to use on a "leaner." Strap up the foot and then lead the horse around on three legs until he learns to balance. Remember, the same thing will have to be done on the other side since horses are "one-sided."

Tying one end of a rope to the horse's foot or ankle strap and the other end around his neck as close to the base as possible is another method. If someone is help-ing you, a better approach is to take the rope from the

91

horse's foot up over his back, bring it down under his belly, and wrap it once around the pastern. Then your helper can stand off to the side and handle the rope, giving and taking as necessary.

A good way to avoid burning either a front or hind foot is to fold a feed sack lengthwise, wiring the ends together. Slip the sack around the horse's pastern and run the rope through this sling.

TYING UP A HIND FOOT

The hind foot may be tied either forward or backward. Tying it back is dangerous, because if the horse falls, he may land on his stifle and be permanently injured. In order to prevent injury after the leg has been tied back, take an old cinch and put it around the leg. Tie a rope to the rings, snug the leg forward and tie the rope to the shoulder. This will also help immobilize the leg if the horse has a tendency to kick.

There are many variations of tying to the tail. A few horses will have so little tail that the foot cannot be tied to it. The problem is to make a knot that will stay in the tail. Some farriers tie an actual knot in the horse's tail as high as possible and then tie a rope above the knot with a clove hitch or slip noose and half-hitches over that. I don't like this method because the knot in the tail is hard to untie. If the horse has a long, thick tail, slip a clove hitch around it at the end of the bone. Pull the hitch as tight as possible, double the rest of the tail over the hitch, and make several half-hitches over everything. I use this method to "head and tail" pack horses.

Another method is to braid an iron ring into the tail

as high as you can. With a ring, a pulley can be made by tying a rope solidly to the ring, putting it down through the "D" ring on the foot strap, and bringing it up through the tail ring again. Then, either tie the rope to the ring with a slip knot or have someone stand behind the horse, giving and taking on the rope as necessary. To put on the foot strap, it may be necessary to tie up a front foot, hobble the front feet, or simply tie the hind foot forward.

To tie a hind foot forward, the old reliable method is the "Scotch hobble." Tie a rope around the base of the horse's neck with a bowline knot, put the rope around his hind pastern, pull the foot forward, and tie the free end to the neck rope with a slip knot. To get the rope under the fetlock, lay the rope beside the horse and make him step over it, or make a loop on the ground, leading him forward until he steps in it.

If you have a helper, put the rope through the neck loop without tying it, bring the end back to the hind foot, and wrap the rope around the pastern. Then have your helper hold the rope off to the side. A slight variation of this method is to take the end of the neck rope under the horse's belly and pull up the opposite hind foot. Be sure to use a cotton rope or put a sack or a piece of split hose on the rope to prevent a rope burn.

I have learned a variation of this method from packers in Idaho that will amaze onlookers. I am sure that anyone who uses this trick a few times will feel that it alone has been worth the price of this book. Make an ankle strap about a foot long with a "D" ring in each end, the object being to put this strap on the pastern without touching the horse's foot. No ropes will touch him, thus avoiding a rope burn. Standing on the horse's right side to tie up the right hind foot, tie one end of the rope (about thirty feet long) around his neck in a bowline. Put the free end through one "D" ring and place it back into the neck rope so it will not be lost. Now slide the strap back so it is at the bight of the rope. Holding the strap, stand behind the horse and get him to step over the doubled rope with his hind foot. Take the free end from the neck rope and run it through the other "D" ring. Pull on the free end, and the strap will slide around his pastern. Bring his foot up and tie the rope end to the neck loop, or put the rope through the loop and have someone hold on to the rope, giving and taking as needed.

If the horse falls down when his foot is tied up, slap him on the belly; if this doesn't work, simply walk away, and he will probably get up by himself.

War Bridles

The object of using a war bridle is to punish the horse only when he misbehaves; steady pressure must never be used, as it will only anger and antagonize him. Horses have a spot directly behind their ears where the nerves are close to the surface, and the war bridle's effectiveness is based on this fact. If not placed over this area, the bridle will not produce the desired effect. Never tie a horse to a solid object while he is wearing a war bridle.

War bridles may be purchased equipped with wide rings on the sides of the bit to keep it from pulling through the mouth and a pulley to exert pressure at the top of the head when the lead strap is jerked.

There are many methods of making a war bridle. If the horse is haltered, the simplest one is to put the lead strap through one of the lower side rings on the halter, under the horse's upper lip, and snap it into the ring on the other side of the halter. This is especially effective if the lead strap has a chain on the end.

A rope may be used to fashion a war bridle by tying a small loop in one end and putting it in the horse's mouth or under his upper lip. Take the free end up over his head, down the other side, and through the loop. Jerking the free end puts pressure behind his ears.

MISCELLANEOUS

When working with a rough horse, always keep your equipment in top condition to avoid an accident. A horse-shoer should always have plenty of ropes—he doesn't have to hang himself. Sash cord is very good as it stays soft and limber and will not burn a horse as a grass or nylon rope would. It also stays free of kinks.

Learn to tie as many knots as possible; the most important ones are the slip knot, bowline, square knot, clove hitch, and, of course, half-hitch.

VII.

Metalwork

S INCE A PRACTICAL KNOWLEDGE of metals is basic to horseshoeing, as well as to many other trades, this chapter will deal with metals in general.

Many times a keg shoe must be changed or modified in order to do the job intended. These small variations can be made with an arc welder or gas welder and do not require special equipment. At times a special shoe must be made when a keg shoe cannot be modified for the purpose. (See Chapter VIII.)

There are many types of iron, steel, and alloys, and each must be handled differently. A metal may be identified by its appearance, feel, melting point, nature of break, and spark test on a grinder. If you have a sample of a known metal, you can compare the sparks. In the case of iron, the shorter the spark length, the more carbon the metal contains and the harder it is. This test does not hold true for alloys of iron. High-carbon steel is seldom used for making a shoe; however, when working with steel, it is important to remember to heat the steel slowly and not above a cherry-red heat, or the crystal structure will be changed and the metal will be ruined. Steel is weakened and breaks more easily *even after* being tempered if heated too hot.

Since you may want to make or repair your own tools, a discussion of steel follows.

TYPES OF STEEL

As the carbon content of iron increases, it becomes more difficult and complicated to handle. Carbon content is often referred to in points of carbon where one point equals .01 per cent. The mild-steel irons of up to .30 per cent carbon are easy to work with and weld. This is the metal used most in horseshoeing except when making tools.

A low-carbon steel has less than .30 per cent carbon, a medium-carbon steel has .30 per cent-.45 per cent carbon, and a high-carbon steel has more than .45 per cent carbon. In general, the more carbon over .30 per cent, the more the welding current and deposition rate will have to be reduced in relation to mild steel.

It is best not to use oxyacetylene flame on the tool steels as the heat causes distortion and will soften hard metal and cause hard zones in annealed metal.

If the carbon content is over .45 per cent, the work must be preheated before welding. When welding, avoid excessive penetration, use low-hydrogen electrodes, and cool slowly.

Steel derives its strength from the size of the grain structure; a fine grain makes the metal strong. This structure is changed by heating and cooling. Low-carbon and high-carbon steel react differently when heated.

When low-carbon steel is heated, grain refinement

97

starts at about 1325°F. and continues to diminish until the metal is heated to a bright red color, or about 1550°F. When the metal is heated beyond this point, the grains begin to grow in size. This continues until melting temperature is reached. Grain size in high-carbon steel changes immediately when reaching 1325°F.; at this point grain size is very small. The size then increases slowly as the temperature of the metal is increased.

Regardless of previous grain size, low-carbon steel will have its finest grain structure at a bright red heat of about 1550°F. and high-carbon steel, at about 1325°F. These temperatures are known as the critical temperatures because heating beyond them increases the grain size. Either fast or slow cooling will hold this fine-grain structure, but rapid cooling will cause the metal to harden.

HEAT INDICATOR CHART

Indicator	Temperature
White	2000°F.
Yellow	1900°F.
Cherry red	1425°F.
Loses magnetic attraction	1333°F.
Solder melts	450°F.
Can barely be held in hand	150°F.

ANNEALING

By gradually heating and cooling, steel will be softened, flexibility increased, and brittleness reduced. This may be necessary before the piece can be drilled or sharpened. Slowly heat the metal to a cherry red that can be seen in the shadow of the room and then bury it in the cinders to let it cool. The metal must be held at heat long enough for the carbon to distribute itself uniformly. This may take several hours for some metals. After it is worked, it may be tempered and brought to the required hardness again. Allowing it to cool, without covering, in cold weather could result in some "air temper" and not give the results desired.

TEMPERING

Metal must contain a certain amount of carbon before it will respond to tempering. Low-carbon steel of only .20 per cent carbon can be hardened to some extent, but it must be cooled extremely fast in iced salt water. Tempering is done in a range from about 1100°F. to 400°F.

TEMPERING CHART

Color	Representative tool	Approximate temperature
Red	Horse rasp	1100°F.
Faint Red	Center punch	900°F.
Brown	Screw driver	700°F.
Purple	Knives and axes	550°F.
Dark Blue	Cold chisels and springs	400°F.
Light Blue	— —	No hardness left

There are three methods of tempering the edge of a tool. The first is simply to heat the tool to a red color and then let it cool to the proper temperature before quenching in a cold liquid. The colors are difficult to distinguish with this method.

99

The second method is to heat the piece back from the edge, and, as the heat conducts, you will be able to see the bands of color moving to the edge. When the proper color reaches the edge of the tool, quench the tool as previously mentioned.

The third method is to heat the tool to a cherry-red heat of about 1400°F. At this point it will lose its magnetic attraction. Now quench the edge to be tempered by moving it up and down in a solution of oil, water, salt water, kerosene, or other comparable liquid. Moving it up and down prevents the formation of a line where the crystalline structure is changed. Remove the tool from the liquid and quickly grind or file the edge so that you can see the bands of color moving toward the tip as the heat is conducted from the center of the tool to the edge. The first color to appear will be blue, the next, purple, etc. Quench the tool at the proper color and move it back and forth in the liquid. Since the edge was first quenched at a red color, it will be extremely hard and brittle. Now as the heat is conducted to the edge, it softens the metal and removes brittleness so that the desired combination of strength and hardness will be achieved.

Always test the tool as soon as it is finished. A little experience with a good sharp file will indicate the necessary hardness. If it is too hard, it will break when used; if it is too soft, it will dull easily. Most tools are hardened so that a new file will barely cut them.

WELDING IN THE FORGE

This is seldom necessary with today's electric and

100

gas welders, which can do a better job; however, there may be times when the forge is the only equipment available.

A forge weld is made at a temperature of about $2500°F$. With this low heat, complete fusion is not obtained as it is with an electric arc or oxyacetylene flame with a temperature in excess of $6000°F$. Also a weld that is hammered together will contain more scale and oxide. Forge welds, however, have sufficient strength for horseshoes.

The secret of a good forge weld is in the fire. Use a good grade of blacksmith coal and plenty of it. Keep the fire banked with wet coal and do not allow the fire to become hollow. As the coke burns, keep pushing the coal in from the outer edge so that it is converted to coke also.

For welding, a clean coke fire without any green coal is needed. Have a clear, concentrated, white flame. Be sure to have five or six inches of coke between your work and the air blast coming in at the bottom, or the cold air will cool the metal and cause it to scale and flake.

Clean the anvil face and have a hammer ready, for the weld must be made quickly when the metal reaches the proper heat.

If, for example, a bar shoe is to be made, the ends will be heated, scarfed, and bent into the desired position. (See the illustration in Chapter VIII.) The shoe is then reheated. If a flux is used, it is applied when the metal reaches a red heat. Now heat the shoe until the surface becomes white and molten; this stage will be accompanied by white sparks. Quickly remove the shoe from the fire, tap it against the anvil to knock off slag, and hammer it, first lightly and then harder, until the pieces are united.

Steel is much more difficult than iron to weld in this manner because it cannot be heated to a white heat. Always use a flux when working with steel and apply the flux without removing the work if possible. If no commercial flux is available, borax is a good substitute.

Hard-surfacing Shoes

Either the gas or arc welder may be used for this purpose. When using an arc welder, keep the rod straight up and down, hold a long arc, and use the lowest heat setting possible in order to avoid getting too much base metal fused with the hard metal.

There are many kinds of hard-surfacing materials. They come in powder, paste, and solid rods. Some of these materials get harder the more they are pounded. There are two general types: one to withstand impact and one to withstand abrasion. For horseshoeing, a combination of these qualities is necessary.

Borium (tungsten carbide) is one of the best hard-surfacing materials for horseshoes. It is the hardest substance that can be deposited by welding and also the most expensive. Hard-surfacing with an arc welder is cheaper; however, I have found that the very best job can be done with gas. The borium to be applied with gas heat comes in long tubes containing large particles of borium, 8–10 screen size in a filler metal. As the softer filler wears away, the large particles give a good grip on concrete or ice.

102

When possible, the shoe should be bent to fit the hoof before it is treated, since a hardened shoe may break. If the shoe has already been treated, it should be heated cherry red before bending it. Use about half the total amount on the toe and one-fourth on each heel to get even wear. When applying, be sure the shoe is clean. It is best to grind the surface first. Heat the shoe until the surface starts to melt and then apply the borium, melting it into the molten shoe. Using an excess of acetylene, wash with flame to make the particles stand out. This is called a carbonizing flame and will actually add a small amount of carbon, which helps to harden the shoe. Let the shoe cool gradually.

This is an expensive process and will double the cost of the shoe; however, since the shoes will wear at least twice as long and give a much better grip, which gives the horse more confidence, the results are well worth the cost.

Don't hammer the hardened metal against the anvil or it will dent the face.

If there is no hard-surface rod available, use cast iron, either the cast-iron welding rod or simply regular melted cast iron, and rub it into the white-hot metal. Cool quickly in water to harden.

ARC WELDER

Every shop should have an electric welder. Although it is possible to weld in the forge or with a gas welder, it is cheaper and faster with an arc welder. With it, you can build up the material, punch holes, and cut the metal.

103

It is a simple matter to fit a regular shoe, cut a bar, and weld it, giving a perfect fit. This is not a simple task in the forge.

D.C. welders have certain advantages over A.C. They are portable if powered by a gasoline engine, often have a 110-volt receptacle for running other electrical equipment, and give a little smoother weld. Further, heat can be regulated somewhat by reversing polarity. A 180-amp. A.C. welder, however, can take care of any job required of a horseshoer.

An A.C. machine is better for thawing out pipes than a D.C. welder, and there is no magnetic-arc blow. In addition to these benefits, an A.C. welder is much less expensive. Either machine must be wired for 220 volts.

Always try to stand on a dry surface when arc welding, wear gloves and protective clothing, and remember that the ultraviolet rays can penetrate your eyelids so always wear a shield.

Since several companies make many types of welding rod, a universal numbering system has been developed. It usually consists of a letter and four numbers, such as E6011 (this one is a general-purpose rod for mild steel). The "E" stands for "electrode" and means that it is an electric and not a gas rod. The first two numbers ("60") stands for "thousand-pounds-per-square-inch" of strength. The third number ("1") stands for position in which the rod may be used (all positions in this case, including flat, horizontal, vertical, or overhead). The fourth number ("1") indicates the type of coating and current which can be used (in this case,

104

either A.C. or D.C.). Here is a list of rods needed for special jobs:

E6011 or E6013, for general purpose
E7018, low-hydrogen rod for welding steel
Aluminum, (manufactured for D.C. only)
Cast iron
Hard-surfacing rod
Stainless steel
Special cutting rods
Sheet metal

With this assortment of rods in several sizes, most jobs can be handled. Keep rods in a dry, clean container.

GAS WELDERS

Electric welding for heavier materials, such as horse-shoes, is faster, cheaper, and more popular than gas; however, gas has certain advantages, such as portability. It may be used anywhere, independent of electricity, and is also better than electricity for cutting.

As with an electric welder, anyone can purchase an outfit and learn to use it by following the instructions. Keep a healthy respect for the gas and follow the rules of safety. Acetylene gas is extremely inflammable; don't use it to start a car or you will probably blow the head off. Since it will explode in the free state, don't try to put it in any container other than the one in which it came. Check the bottle, gauges, and line frequently for leaks. Oxygen is generally thought of as a harmless gas, but it will explode under certain conditions, such as coming in contact with oil or grease. *Don't oil the gauges.*

Always crack the valve to blow dust and dirt out before attaching the gauges to the tank or else a gauge may explode. Three factors must be present for an explosion to take place: fuel, oxygen, and heat. If dust is blown through the small valve in the gauge, it creates friction, causing heat. The oxygen and fuel, in this case the metal gauge, are already present—and *boom!*

The general rule to follow is to set the gauges so that twice as much oxygen pressure as acetylene pressure is used. Don't use over 15 pounds acetylene pressure.

Propane may be used instead of acetylene, but different gauges are required. It does not burn as hot as acetylene; however, it can be used for welding, and it is good for cutting. It also has the advantage of being much more economical than acetylene.

In my horseshoeing outfit I carry a small bottle of acetylene. It is cheaper in a large bottle for shop use.

Welding may be done with a rod (baling wire makes a very good rod for mild steel) or without a rod, where the pieces are simply melted together.

Brazing is simply heating the iron until it is so hot that the brass rod will flow on evenly; the base metal is not melted. Brazing is used either for joining or coating. It is the process which is used on the parade shoe mentioned in Chapter XI to make the shoe a bright gold.

As you gain skill, you will want a full assortment of rod on hand, including mild steel, brass, pot metal, hard-surfacing metal, cast iron, aluminum, and stainless steel.

Carbon Arc

For the person who cannot spend a large sum for

forge, arc, and gas welder, there is an acceptable substitute. For about fifteen dollars, a carbon arc can be bought that will act as a portable forge for bending, heating heels for trimming, and light welding. It is very good for soldering and brazing and can replace the gas welder for welding with a rod. A carbon arc makes concentrated heat and it does not "blow" like the gas torch. Work can often be done with less distortion, and the material being prepared does not need to be grounded as with an arc welder.

There is one model that plugs into an arc welder, so that, if you have an arc welder and a carbon arc, you can get along without a gas welder. An A.C. machine is best as one carbon tends to get too hot with D.C.

There are other welding processes, such as inert-gas welding, which have advantages, especially for nonferrous metals and their alloys. No doubt these methods will become more widely used in the future because of the increasing popularity of alloys.

VIII.

Handmade Shoes

Few men have the skill or equipment to make a shoe out of a piece of iron; therefore, I would like to discuss the subject at length as it is a skill that should not be lost.

Making the Shoe

Almost any size or shape of iron or steel may be used, but for an ordinary shoe, a piece of mild steel ¾-inch by 5/16-inch by 12-inch long is about right. This would make a No. 0 shoe. The length will vary according to the size of the foot, and the rule to follow is: after preparing the hoof for the shoe, measure from the toe to the angle the bars make with the wall (buttress), then double this and add 1 inch.

The parts of a horseshoe are:
  a. The toe is that portion between the front nail holes.
  b. A branch is half of the shoe, from the toe to the heel.
  c. The quarter is that part between the last nail hole and the heel.

d. The heels are the ends of the branches.

e. The lower surface is the ground surface.

f. The upper surface is the foot surface, having two parts—the bearing surface, which supports the wall, and the concave surface, which is beaten down so that it does not put pressure on the sole.

An expert can make a shoe in one heat; however, the beginner should use at least three heats, one for the toe and one for each branch.

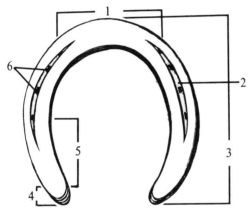

NORMAL SHOE

1—*Toe*

2—*Crease*

3—*Branch*

4—*Heel*

5—*Quarter*

6—*Nail holes*

This picture illustrates a normal front shoe. Note the placement of the nail holes. They are set farther in at the toe than at the heel and are confined to the front half of the shoe.

109

Heat the center of the bar to a cherry red. Pick up one end with a pair of tongs and remove the bar from the fire. Place the other end on the face of the anvil; and with the round face of the rounding hammer, strike the center of the bar, hammering toward yourself, until an oval turn is made and the branches form a right angle for a front shoe. For a hind shoe, bend the iron until the angle is more acute. As the metal bends, it thickens on the inside. Lay the shoe flat on the anvil and make the toe even in thickness.

Heat one of the branches and narrow it from the middle of the quarter to the heel by placing it edgewise on the face of the anvil and pounding it with overlapping blows. This thickens the branch, so lay the shoe flat and level it. The branch is now ready to bend to shape.

Front shoes and hind shoes are made differently. To make a front shoe, after the toe is bent and the quarter narrowed, place it over the anvil horn and, pounding lightly where the shoe extends over the horn, keep pushing it onto the horn, at the same time moving it down the horn toward the small end. This gives a rounded shape to the branch. When making a hind shoe, do not move it down the horn and do not round the branch all the way to the heel. Instead, straighten the branch from the toe about halfway to the heels, then bend the rest of the branch to fit the heel. This gives a more pointed toe to fit a hind foot.

Before punching the nail holes, make a crease in the shoe with a chisel, special fullering tool, or a forepunch to make a groove in which to countersink the nailheads.

The nail holes are made next. One of the important

110

features of a handmade shoe is that placement of holes can be adjusted to avoid cracks and other defects in the hoof. Also the distance of the nail holes from the outside of the shoe can be varied according to the thickness of the wall. One of the bad features of a keg shoe is that, when the shoe is bent to fit the hoof (as indicated by the white line), the outer wall may have to be dubbed off so that it corresponds to the outer border of the shoe. If the nails were set in farther, this would not be necessary. The wall is thicker at the toe than at the heels; therefore, the nail holes must be graduated too.

The first hole is punched about an inch to the rear of a line drawn parallel to the toe of the shoe and three-eighths of an inch or more from the outer edge (see the illustration at the beginning of this chapter). The rest of the nails are then spaced out as needed and graduated until the last nail is only one-quarter of an inch or less from the outer edge of the shoe. The pritchel is driven through while the shoe is held directly over the pritchel hole in the anvil. A tap on the edge of the shoe will remove the burr against the pritchel hole. The forepunch must be the same size as the head of the nail, and the point of the pritchel must correspond to the size of nail about two-thirds of the distance up its shank, insuring a tight fit. The holes must be pritcheled at the same angle as the wall at the point where they will be driven. This means that the holes will be graduated in degree, the front holes being quite slanted and the heel holes being almost straight up. Hold the pritchel out at an angle for the toe hole and make it straighter for each hole until it is about straight up for the heel hole.

111

Once good, clean nail holes of the same size are made, the heels are cut to fit the foot. Mark the heels, heat them to a white heat, and place them horizontally on the hardy with the foot surface up and at a 45-degree angle so that the outer edge is longer. When the cut is almost completed and a dark line is showing, strike away from yourself so that the hardy is not dulled with the hammer. Now place the shoe in a vise and hot-rasp the heels.

With the foot surface up, use the rounding hammer to seat out the inside so that the sole does not bear on the shoe. Do not go too far past the quarter or the bars will not be able to support their share of the shoe.

The shoe must now be leveled. If the rounded face of the rounding hammer is used to concave the foot surface, the shoe will be almost level. Turn it over so that the ground surface is up, and make light, overlapping blows all around the shoe with the flat face of the hammer. A dark heat may be used for this step.

Making handmade shoes is good basic experience. Soon you will be able to look at a horse's foot and bend a shoe that will fit or be very close almost every time. A man can be justly proud of himself when he attains this skill.

Clips and Their Use

Clips are not needed on a regular shoe applied to a normal foot, and there is no reason to spend extra time on them.

Clips should be used, however, to hold cracks together, especially at the toe where a clip on each side of the crack is a real aid. They are important on shoes with extensions or trailers, in which case they are put on the same side as the projection to keep the shoe from being driven across the foot. They are also used in rough country or on shoes with high calks. Heel clips are useful for horses that have injured their heels or that suffer from overexpansion, and they may help to hold a shoe on a dry, brittle foot. A long, thin toe clip can be used for decorative purposes. A high clip is of no additional advantage as the strain is on its base, and this is where the clip must be strong.

Make the clips no more than twice the thickness of the shoe height. A long clip could be bent down and cut the opposite leg, or it could puncture the sole if the shoe came loose and the horse stepped on it. If a pad is used, the clip should be made larger than normal.

A clip may be drawn from the shoe itself or welded

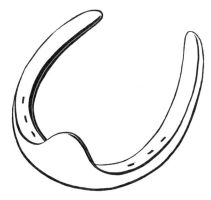

SHOE WITH TOE CLIP

onto the shoe. One-eighth-inch sheet iron makes good clips. If drawn from the shoe, the metal may be taken from either the ground surface or the bearing surface. To do this, heat the metal almost white, place it about a quarter of an inch over the edge of the anvil (or horn clip if there is one) at a 45° angle, and draw the metal out by using the rounded face of the rounding hammer. Make the first blow a hard one in order to seat the shoe against the anvil. When the metal is drawn out, place the shoe over the horn and bend it up to conform to the angle of the wall.

The clip should be set into the wall slightly, especially at the toe. It should not be burned in, although a hot clip will mark the area that should be cut out to receive it. Never place a clip over or near a sore area on the hoof, and when setting the clip, don't hit it too hard, for it could cause a tumor of the wall.

CALKS

Calks are projections on the bottom of the shoe and are used for many purposes. They are used primarily to give the horse footing or to change the angle of the foot. Ice calks are discussed in Chapter XI.

By changing the angle, you can change the speed of the break-over, relieve strain on tendons, etc. Calks may also be used to help the foot make a straight flight by acting as a brake to straighten the foot as it lands. Calks which are slightly turned outward help to give lateral support to the heels. This is especially helpful in narrow-footed horses and mules. Calks will also prolong the life of the shoe.

A toe calk should rarely be used on a saddle horse. If a toe calk is used, the farther it is set back from the toe, the quicker the foot will break over. Since the hind feet are the propelling force, heel calks may have some advantage here. Also, on front feet with a very long toe, heel calks or swelled heels will give a better angle to the feet.

For the horses that work on their hind legs, the following combination of calks works very well. The inside heel can be fitted with a diamond-shape calk or swelled heel, while the outside heel has a regular-turned calk. Then, as the horse turns to the left, most of the weight is on the left hind leg; the outside heel calk acts as a pivot and the inside diamond calk slides easily. Also, this type of calk on the inside of the hoof is less likely to cause a tread wound on the opposite foot.

Calks should never be used except for a special purpose, such as that mentioned above. They have many bad features, but it is difficult to change the minds of people who have never used anything else. A plate shoe is much closer to the natural hoof and allows greater freedom of action.

Calks may change the natural position of the bones, thereby increasing the effects of concussion. They are subject to snagging and increase stumbling, inflict wounds on the horse wearing them as well as on other horses, catch in wire and halters, and may interfere with balance just as high heels on a woman's shoe. A toe calk reduces lateral support at the toe and may slow the break-over of the front foot enough to cause the hind foot to hit it. In rear shoes, calks make it hard to point

115

the toe of the shoe enough to fit a pointed hoof. Heel calks keep the frog off of the ground and thereby reduce the blood supply to the foot, since a healthy frog acts as a heart in each foot to pump the blood. If the frog is elevated so that it cannot perform its natural functions, it will waste away and cause contracted heels. The more the frog is used, the larger and healthier it becomes. In general, flat shoes prolong the useful life of the horse by promoting sound feet.

TRAILERS

A trailer is a prolongation of a branch. Trailers are usually bent out at a 45° angle at the end of the heel. They are used for two purposes—as a lateral support and as a brake to shorten the stride or slightly turn the toe. For example, if the horse's toes point outward, he will break over and generally land on the inside of the hoofs. A trailer is placed on each inside branch. As the heels come into contact with the ground, the trailer will strike first and pivot the toe slightly so that it lands straighter. If the hoof lands straight, it will be in a position to break over the center of the toe when it leaves the ground. Experimenting will show the best location for a trailer and how much bend is needed to produce the best results.

If a trailer is used on the inside branch, it should be very short; a low calk under it may help. I would put a bell boot on the opposite pastern of a horse shod with an inside trailer and leave it on until I was satisfied with the effect.

Simply leaving both branches long will help to slow

116

down the foot by the same type of braking action and will give support to the rear tendons.

Trailers cannot be used on the front feet if the horse is to be worked fast as he will catch them with his hind feet and tear the shoe off. The exception would be a long-backed horse, but even then I would slow down the hind feet by lowering the heels as much as possible and leaving the branches long.

When making a trailer, bend it *at the end of the heel* and be sure the heel is properly supported.

Never turn a horse with a trailer loose while he is wearing a halter, or he might try to scratch his head, thus getting the trailer caught on the halter. A few seconds spent taking the halter tab out of the hole may save digging a larger hole—*for the horse.*

EXTENSIONS AND SQUARE TOES

Extensions are elongations placed on the shoe to make the hoof break over at the center of the toe. This makes the foot fly straight. A square-toed shoe is used for the same purpose and also speeds break over slightly. Don't set this shoe farther back than the white line.

The point of the extension should be placed where the hoof is breaking over. The break-over point will be apparent if the horse is wearing old shoes as they will be worn where the hoof breaks over. The shoe will wear on the low side of the toe when breaking over and landing. The foot breaks over the low side. This will be on the outside for toe-in or base-narrow feet and on the inside for cow-hocked, splayfooted, or toe-out feet.

A 5/16-inch round rod works very well for extensions

117

Cut off the amount needed, bend in a right angle, and weld on the extension where the foot has been breaking over. It is best to fit the shoe first if possible.

The break-over can also be changed by rolling the toe of the shoe on the side opposite the extension or by welding a bar diagonally across the break-over point. This bar can be tapered from the outside toward the toe to help roll the foot over the center of the toe.

If the trouble is caused by something other than the foot, an extension will probably not do much good. Usually extensions do not show any effect except at high speeds.

Extensions should be used with care on the inside of the shoe as they can injure the opposite leg.

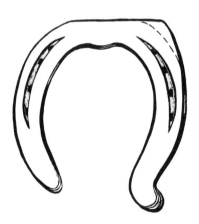

CORRECTIVE SHOE

Bar Shoes

Bar shoes are used to apply pressure to the frog in diseases such as contracted heels and to prevent such pressure in navicular disease, etc., to protect injuries to the heels and sole area, to hold a pad or medication under the foot, and to strengthen the shoe. Extra weight can be placed in the bar if needed.

Hot shoe blanks have long branches that may be bent in and welded together. To do this, scarf the ends (see illustration below), bend the branches *at the end of the heels,* and overlap as shown. (See the section on "Welding in the Forge" in Chapter VII.)

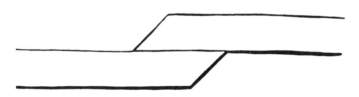

BAR PREPARED FOR FORGE WELD

When using an electric or gas welder, do not overlap the ends but simply bring them together.

A bar shoe can be made from a regular keg shoe by fitting it to the hoof and then welding in a bar. With this method, the bar can be set forward or back, depending on where it is needed. When making a handmade bar shoe, measure the trimmed hoof, as described earlier in this chapter, add the distance across the buttresses, and start with the necessary amount of iron. The bar

119

may be modified as needed (see descriptions of the three-quarter bar, drop bar, and rest shoe in Chapter IX).

Frog pressure can be regulated by the use of leather fillers bolted to the bar. If the frog is depressed about a quarter of an inch when the shoe is nailed on, it usually will be about right.

IX

Diseases, Injuries, and Other Ailments

T HE PURPOSE OF THIS CHAPTER is to supply general information to horsemen concerning prevention and treatment of disorders that affect the horse's locomotion. I have mentioned something about the cause, detection, and treatment of each defect in addition to recommending shoeing corrections in order to give the horseshoer the basic information necessary to make a decision in each case. It is not meant to replace a veterinarian's advice but is to be used in conjunction with the veterinarian's recommendations to help the horse as much as possible.

Many of today's veterinarians do not understand the use of horseshoes as an aid to healing and correction of disease. Many of those that do don't know where to have the shoes made when they do need them. Directions included here will be of assistance to the local metalworker. With this in mind, I will go into each of the common diseases and discuss the basic points, with an emphasis on shoeing corrections. Locating the lameness is discussed in Chapter I; however, if there is a specific test for a certain disease, I have tried to include it here.

GENERAL PROBLEMS

Sometimes horses are said to be "stove up" or to have "gone bad in the feet." In many cases examination and testing will not indicate any specific lameness. In my opinion, this problem has two principal causes: either the foot is too dry and is putting pressure on sensitive parts ("hoof bound") or the feet are simply too small— a foot of any given size can support only so much weight.

Handling dry feet is discussed in Chapter I and is fairly easy to rectify. If the problem is not treated, it can lead to serious complications, which may be more dangerous and expensive than the initial disorder.

When more weight is applied to a horse's hoofs than they are capable of carrying, they will, in time, begin to ache, and the horse will become susceptible to other diseases and disorders if worked too hard. A small foot has little area over which to distribute concussion, and, therefore, the effect of concussion is increased. Thoroughbred and Quarter Horse breeders, in my opinion, have been especially negligent in breeding for adequate foot sizes. Other factors could also be involved in this problem, such as very thin walls and sole, a frog that is too small, etc. If a horse is allowed to mature before he is worked heavily, he will be useful much longer than a horse that is not fully developed.

Another factor influencing foot development is nutrition. For horses, the ratio of calcium to phosphorus should be about one to one. Tests have shown that, when this ratio reaches one to two or more, changes in the

122

skeletal parts are likely to occur. A veterinarian may advise you to feed the horse a phosphorus mineral or to see that he gets more sunlight (Vitamin D) if he is stabled. I believe that future research will show nutrition to be more important in diseases such as ringbone than is now commonly believed.

Concussion directly or indirectly influences almost everything that goes wrong with the legs and feet. It cannot be overemphasized, therefore, that the horse should not be forced to run on a hard surface, especially a young horse, and that the feet should be trimmed and shod properly.

Concussion or an injury sets up an inflammation in the periosteum, which is the membrane that covers the bone. The inflammation causes an increased blood supply to the area, and if this continues for any length of time, ossification, which is the deposit of lime and other substances, occurs. The results of this process are the enlargements seen in cases of ringbone, bone spavin, etc. The horseshoer can be responsible for starting this inflammation by trimming the feet out of balance (higher on one side than the other) so that an unnatural strain is put on the tendons where they are attached to the bone. Every horseshoer should be aware of this fact and have the utmost respect for the dire results of improper trimming.

A common treatment in the past that is still used is "firing." A hot iron is applied to the area, creating an acute inflammation, and, as this heals, it *may* also heal the initial local inflammation. It can also make it worse, and usually leaves a blemish. The use of counterirritants, injections, and surgery are replacing firing in much of today's practice.

If treatment is started immediately after injury, the horse has a much better chance of recovery. In many cases prolonged rest offers the only chance for permanent recovery. The use of cold and heat is an important method of initial treatment. Cold treatments are used first to prevent swelling, and hot treatments are used later to reduce swelling.

If one leg is so sore that the horse cannot carry any weight on it, the opposite hoof may founder or break down under the additional strain. To prevent this, the horse should be hung in a sling, or special care should be given to the sound hoof. This would include removing the shoe and trimming the hoof, seeing that the hoof contains the proper amount of moisture, bedding the horse properly, and applying cold water occasionally to tone up the blood vessels.

Generally a keg shoe can be modified to do the job, and only in special cases will a handmade shoe be required. If a handmade shoe is used, it should be kept as simple as possible and still obtain the desired results.

ARTHRITIS

Basically, arthritis is the inflammation of a joint, and may involve any of the bones, ligaments, or synovial capsules. It may become chronic and infection may result from it. Enlargement of the joint usually occurs from increased production of synovia (lubricating

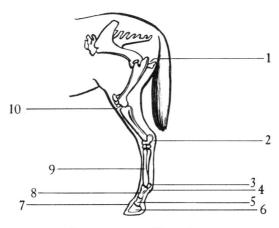

BONES OF THE HIND LEG

1—*Hip joint*

2—*Hock*

3—*Sesamoid bone*

4—*Fetlock*

5—*Short Pastern*

6—*Coffin bone*

7—*Coronet*

8—*Long pastern*

9—*Cannon bone*

10—*Stifle joint*

fluid), increased blood supply, and new bone growth or tissue thickening.

If bone changes have not occurred, the horse should have complete rest for several months—six months or more in severe cases. Follow the veterinarian's instructions.

Once bone damage has occurred, the only cure may be the growing together of the bones involved, called ankylosis. When this union of the bones has taken place, the horse may be serviceable and without pain, although his movement will be somewhat restricted. The shoe for a horse with ankylosis should have a rocked toe to make breaking over easier. (A rocked toe is actually bent up, while a rolled toe has a rounded bottom edge.)

Bog Spavin

Bog spavin is a round, smooth, well-defined, fluctuating enlargement on the front and inside of the hock. It is caused by overwork, concussion, blows, injuries, and slipping. When, for one of these reasons, excess synovial fluid is secreted, the result is a bulging of the capsular ligament covering the joint.

Treatment should include rest, application of counter-irritants, and use of a high-heeled shoe.

Bone Spavin

Bone spavin is a bony deposit on the hock. It is generally on the inside and front of the leg and is always serious. The degree to which the horse's usefulness will be impaired, however, depends largely upon the location of the deposit. It the spavin is high on the hock, it may not affect the horse's movement as much as it would if it directly involved the joint, especially the internal bone surfaces (blind spavin). In other words, the degree of seriousness is not always in direct proportion to the size of the enlargement. When the horse has blind spavin, the hock may appear normal; the problem, however, will show up if the hock is X-rayed.

There are many causes of spavin. Anything that produces an inflammation of the hock can develop into

126

spavin. Here again, concussion or excessive strain are the principal agents; sickle-hocked horses (see Chapter X) are very susceptible to this disease.

Even before any swelling occurs, lameness may be evident. Usually the horse will be lame when he starts moving in the morning; but after some exercise, his gait will improve, and may show no defect. Lameness is more persistent in blind spavin. The leg will probably improve little with use, and it may worsen instead. When resting, the horse will point the toe. When in motion, the leg will be advanced in a rigid position, and the toe will catch on the ground, causing wear at the toe.

Spavin can be detected by grasping the leg just above the fetlock, lifting it high under the horse's stomach, and holding it there for about three minutes. Then drop the foot and walk the horse immediately. If spavin exists, the lameness will be greatly intensified and the horse will try to walk on his toe.

A veterinarian can perform surgery on the ligaments involved, and this will aid in relieving the pain. However, the horse's gait will always be somewhat impaired. The most effective cure is the growing together of the bones

SPAVIN SHOE
(*side view*)

127

in the joint, with, it is hoped, a minimum of impairment. To accomplish this the leg must be placed in a cast.

Lower the toe as much as possible when shoeing a horse with this ailment. Use very high heels, preferably a sloping-wedge heel so that it will not have a tendency to catch in the ground and cause discomfort.

To help roll the foot over the inside toe, thereby relieving strain on the inside of the hock, use a long calk. Start on the outside of the shoe and gradually bevel the calk until it is flush with the shoe at the inside of the toe. Hold the leg as low as possible while shoeing.

Capped Elbow

Often called a "shoe boil," this problem involves swelling at the point of the elbow, caused by any repeated irritation of the elbow. The swelling may become quite large and even pussy. Capped elbow is most commonly caused when the horse strikes his elbow on the floor as he puts his front feet under him in the effort to rise from a lying position. Also, when he is lying down, the heels or heel calks on the front shoe may strike the elbow; usually the damage is done by the inside branch of the shoe. Other causes include the rider's boot continually tapping the elbow or the belly band of a harness rubbing the elbow.

If the horse is kept in a stall, provide a good, deep bed. Fit the front shoes up to the last bearing point of the wall and rasp the heels smooth. The inside branch may be shortened slightly. While the elbow is healing, fold a sack and strap it to the leg just below the fetlock. This

128

will prevent the foot or shoe from hitting the elbow and irritating it further.

CONTRACTED HEELS

A hoof in this condition becomes contracted and shrinks to less than its normal size; this problem appears primarily in the heels or the quarters. I hate to see contracted heels because this usually means that the horse is being neglected or that he has been subject to careless and incorrect shoeing.

Contracted heels are caused by letting the feet dry out (sawdust or peat moss will draw moisture), leaving the heels too high when trimming, trimming the foot unevenly, cutting out the bars or the frog, and putting the nails too far back in the hoof. Contraction also develops from using high calks, leaving the shoe on so long that the high wall holds the frog off of the ground, and paring the sole, thus allowing it to dry out and draw the heels inward. Lack of exercise and disease or injury also contribute to contraction.

If the contraction is caused by disease, it usually appears in the lame foot only. More than one foot will be affected, however, if the problem results from poor care. Contraction generally develops in the front feet, although the hind feet can also be affected. Frequently only one quarter, usually the inner one, is contracted. A foot in a "broken in" condition will cause the inside quarter to contract. More weight is then placed on the low side of the hoof, causing it to curl under and contract even more.

To check for contraction, measure the distance across

129

the buttresses; this should not be less than the distance across the foot at a point that is one inch back from the toe.

When treatment is started, the outline of the foot should be traced on a piece of cardboard so that progress can be checked. In new cases the heels should be lowered and the unshod horse turned out into a wet pasture for a few weeks. With correct care and shoeing, he will have no further trouble. In cases where the feet are dry, they must be moistened before anything else will be very effective.

Further treatment will be along two basic lines, or a combination of the two. The first is to spread the heels mechanically, and the second is to spread the heels using pressure on the frog. Neither method should be tried until the foot is moist. If the feet are very dry, the horse should stand in water or mud for half a day every day for about a week.

The most common shoe used for this problem is a bevel-edged shoe. The branches are beveled on the foot surface up to one-eighth of an inch from the inside to the outside of the branch. Too much of a bevel could actually split the heels, so don't try to correct the contraction all at once; let the foot expand slowly. The shoe should be wide at the heels so that as the foot expands, it will be supported by the shoe. Sometimes the wall at the heels is rasped thin or grooves cut in the wall so that it will expand more readily. Don't use this method unless the feet can be kept moist, or the thin walls will dry out, counteracting any beneficial effect.

Another aid to expansion is to cut the toe of the shoe

about halfway through from the inside; then every few weeks pry the heels slightly apart. A special tool is available for this job. Keep the foot extremely moist and soft to make this method effective.

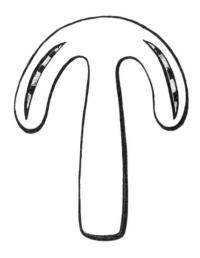

THE "T" SHOE

The natural way to expand the heels is to put pressure on the frog. There are several types of shoes that will do this. A "T" shoe has a bar which conforms to the shape of the frog. If needed, leather fillers can be bolted on until they put pressure on the frog when the shoe is nailed in place. The T-bar shoe may be used with full branches and beveled edges if this will do more good than actually having the heels make contact with the ground.

131

REAR VIEW OF DROP-BAR SHOE

A "drop-bar" shoe may also be used. A bar, shaped to put pressure on the frog, is welded between the rear branches. Leather fillers may be bolted to this bar also since it is difficult to put the dropped bar in the exact position for maintaining pressure when the shoe is nailed on the hoof. Depressing the frog about a quarter of an inch when the shoe is on will usually be sufficient.

Another useful shoe is a three-quarter shoe, in which the branches come only to the quarters. This shoe is set *into* the wall so that it is level with the wall at the quarters. In this way the shoe will keep the foot from becoming tender and yet will not interfere with expansion at the heels.

Additional treatments involve the application of counterirritants on the heels to increase circulation, growth, and speed of recovery, and the use of an artificial frog, made by rolling a large ball of oakum and placing it over the frog and under a pad.

CORNS

Pododermatitis circumscripta—remember this name, and you can impress your friends or your veterinarian. A corn is a bruise on the sensitive part of the horse's hoof, located in the angle between the wall and the bar.

132

A bruised sole differs from a corn in that it is located anywhere else on the sole and tends to grow out and be replaced by new horn.

Corns are of two types, wet and dry. Pus will be present in a wet (suppurating) corn. If the pus is thin and grey, it is not too serious, but should be treated and watched. However, if it is thick and yellow, it is quite serious, and a veterinarian should be called. Such a corn may become chronic or damage the foot permanently. A dry corn is usually red; however, the color of the corn varies somewhat with the color of the foot. If bright red blood is apparent, the bruise is a new corn; if it is dark and dry, it is an old corn.

If the sensitive laminae of the wall have been injured, the discoloration will be *at* the white line. Otherwise, it will be restricted to the angle of the buttresses or sole.

Corns are caused by anything that crushes or bruises the sensitive laminae, such as lowering the heels too much, cutting out the bars, crushing the sole when the old shoe is pulled, or fitting the shoe so that it presses on the sole. Unbalanced feet, shoes that are not level, dryness, contracted heels, or debris wedged between the shoe and sole also cause corns. In some cases, shoes left on too long may cause corns because the shoe grows forward with the foot, allowing the heels to press on the sole. This does not happen, however, unless the shoe is bent since, as the hoof grows forward, it also grows down, keeping the shoe away from the sole. When nails are driven too far toward the heels, thus limiting expansion, it is possible for the wings of the pedal bone

133

to bruise the sensitive sole if the foot is subjected to extreme concussion.

Corns generally appear on the front feet since they carry more weight than the hind feet do, especially when the horse is being ridden. Corns also appear more frequently on the inside of the foot, which is set a little more toward the horse's center of gravity and receives slightly more concussion. The inside wall is also a little straighter, allowing less expansion.

A corn can develop into a very serious problem if not treated early.

Symptoms of corns are a short, choppy stride and pointing the foot when at rest. The horse will try to walk on the outside of the hoof or on the toe, depending upon the location of the corn. Apply pressure *carefully* around the sole with a pair of pinchers or hoof testers, and the horse will flinch when the corn is touched. Horses with short pasterns and with high-heeled, straight-walled feet are predisposed to corns as their feet receive more concussion and have less built-in expansion to dissipate shock.

When treating a corn, see that the foot is moist and soft. The corn should be pared out until a drop of blood appears and then soaked in an antiseptic bath. If the corn is extremely tender, a veterinarian should be called to administer treatment. Do not let the shoe put any pressure over the corn.

It may be necessary to lower the wall and bar over the affected area and use a bar shoe to give the added strength and protection needed. A leather or felt pad packed with pine tar and oakum under the shoe will further protect the corn. A piece of one-half-inch felt absorbs the shock better and does not dry out as quickly as leather.

When trimming the feet, *always lower the sole where the wall and bar make an angle* (buttresses), and the horse will have fewer corns.

THREE-QUARTER-BAR SHOE FOR CORNS

CRACKS

There are two types of cracks, and treatment is somewhat different for each. One type grows from the coronet downward and is sometimes called a false quarter; the other grows from the bottom of the wall upward. They are classed as toe, quarter, or heel cracks.

Cracks may appear anywhere in the hoof; however, they are found mainly in the inner quarters of the forefeet, toes of the hind feet, and sometimes in the outer

135

quarters of the forefeet. Cracks are caused by dryness and flares, heels that are cut too low, and injuries to the coronet, which is the horn-producing area.

The first step in treating a crack is to immobilize and reinforce the break. The second step is to make sure that the foot contains the proper amount of moisture, and this may mean soaking the foot. To stop a crack that begins at the bottom of the hoof, heat a thin piece of iron to a dark heat and burn it into the hoof at the top of the crack and at right angles to it. A quarter-inch rod may be used to burn the hole, or if no heat is available, drill into the hoof. The object is to burn or drill almost through the wall but not into the sensitive tissues. Remember that the wall is thinner at the quarters than at the toe.

A common treatment is to file a groove across the top of the crack with the corner of the rasp, but this does not go deep enough to do any good except in very shallow cracks. In fact, it does harm because the area dries out after being rasped.

If the crack is the result of injury to the coronet, the hoof will always be defective because, once injured, the horn secreting cells can never completely repair themselves. If the crack originates at the bottom of the hoof and is stopped, it will then grow down with the wall and disappear completely in time. The crack disappears sooner at the quarters than at the toe because the wall is lower.

If the crack is deep and the edges move, the sides must be immobilized. The veterinarian may recommend postponing treatment until lameness subsides. If so, defective shoeing treatment will show up that would not be noticed if the horse was already lame when shod. If the sensitive tissue is protruding through the crack, the veterinarian will probably burn it off. Use a full-bar shoe and side clips to stop expansion. Make the bar narrow and set it far back so that there is no pressure on the frog. Trim the frog before nailing on the shoe. It may be necessary to punch another hole in the shoe so that a nail can be driven behind the crack. Keep the foot moist and give the horse prolonged rest.

There are several ways of immobilizing cracks. The simplest, especially for a toe crack, is to drive a nail across the crack (flat side of the nail out), cut off both ends, and bend the ends into the middle. This should be done about every inch along the crack. It usually helps to heat the pritchel and burn a small hole on each side of the crack. Start the nail in one hole, aiming it to come out the other. If the wall is spread apart, insert a copper wire through the holes and twist together to close the crack. Since quarter cracks do not lend themselves to this method as well as toe cracks, a thin metal plate is made that overlaps the quarter crack and several holes are drilled in each side. After the plate is bent to the pitch of the wall, place it over the crack and burn it into the wall to seat it. Then screw the plate to the hoof with one-quarter-inch wood screws. If the crack extends into the sensitive tissues, pack it with cotton saturated with iodine and drill a hole near the top of the plate to enable you to add more iodine about once a week. A hypodermic syringe works well for adding the iodine. In severe cases, use antibiotics, to retard infection. A poultice may be used around the foot to draw the poison. A large overshoe works well for this.

When nailing the shoe on, never drive nails across a crack. If one of the holes falls over a crack when the shoe is fitted, rivet a nail in that hole in order to seal it. When the toe is cracked, draw a clip up on each side of the toe. Always use a flat shoe and make sure that no weight is on the crack. This can be done by removing some of the wall below the crack or by making a depression in the shoe itself. If the wall is cut out, it should be removed from in front of the crack to a distance that is perpendicular to the top of the crack. This area should be cleaned daily with a hacksaw blade so that dirt does not accumulate and put pressure on the wall.

WALL LOWERED BELOW THE CRACK

A bar shoe gives the maximum amount of support for healing, and counterirritants applied to the coronet hasten the development of new, sound horn.

There are some general points about cracks to remember. A toe crack is closed when weight is placed on the hoof and is open when it is not; a quarter crack is closed when weight is removed from the hoof and open when weight is applied. If the crack is in the front portion of the hoof, lower the heels. If the crack is in the quarters, lower the toe. It is possible for a crack to start on the inside of the wall, in this case only a slight depression will be visible.

Trimming the foot out of balance has been recommended by some writers, but I do not recommend this treatment. By lowering the side having the crack, concussion is reduced all right, but the low side will be carrying most of the weight. It also puts a tremendous strain on the leg, resulting in inflammation and bony growths.

A new treatment is being used which certainly looks good to me—the crack is glued together. To use this method, rest the horse until lameness disappears. First, the feet are soaked if they are dry. Then the crack is cleaned, grooved out, roughened with sandpaper, and glued with epoxy glue. The foot is put in a sling overnight and a heat lamp is used to harden the glue. A foot handled in this manner and then shod as described above has every chance to return to normal.

CURB

Curb is the name given an outward bulge at the back of the hock. Usually the large ligament at the rear of the hock has been strained and has become inflamed and thickened. Sometimes the tendons or their sheaths are involved, and if the bulge is within two inches of the point of the hock, is is possible that one of the hock bones has slipped slightly out of place and is pressing against the tendons.

The usual causes are a violent effort, slipping, a blow at the hock, or kicking the tail gate of a trailer. Horses with faulty hock conformation, such as sickle-hocked horses and horses with narrow hocks, are more prone to curb than other horses. On a normal horse, the area of the leg from the hock to the fetlock will lie in a straight line.

Counterirritants or firing as described earlier may be of some benefit. If treatment is started immediately upon injury, cold applications should be made to keep the swelling down. Horses with good conformation have a much better chance of recovery than do those with weak hocks.

When shoeing, the heels should be raised by sloping wedge heels, thus allowing the foot to slide along. The wedge heels will not catch as ordinary calks do. Use a wide-bearing surface at the heels, roll the toe slightly, and keep the branches long. Never use a toe calk as its resistance retards free action and counteracts the effect of raised heels.

FOUNDER

Founder, or laminitis, is an inflammation of the foot. The sensitive laminae become congested with blood and severe pain results from the pressure, especially at the toe, where the laminae are longest. Founder may be acute or chronic and may involve any or all of the feet, but the problem is most severe when located in the front hoofs.

Most horsemen associate founder with overeating or improper feeding. It is also caused by concussion, overwork, spoiled hay or grain, lush grass, and hard use immediately after trimming long feet. Allowing a hot horse to drink or wade in cold water can also produce this condition. All of the causes are not known; however, the disease can be transmitted through the stomach contents of an affected horse.

A rather common problem is grass founder. Never turn a horse that has been on dry pasture or hay into lush grass and allow him to eat all he wants; let him get used to it gradually. This is especially true if the pasture contains alfalfa or clover. Fat ponies and horses are particularly susceptible to this disease. Once a horse has had an attack, he will be vulnerable to future attacks and should never be allowed to become too fat.

Founder is quite common, and anything that upsets the circulation can cause it, since the foot does not have the safety valve of perspiration to relieve threatened congestion. Many cases go unnoticed if the congestion is relieved before inflammation becomes severe enough to cause lameness or hoof changes.

Always check for founder before buying a horse by trimming the sole of a front foot down to live horn and examining the condition of the white line at the toe.

The main symptom of acute or simple founder is increased heat in the sole, wall, and coronet. Watch the position of the horse's legs; if all four feet are affected, he will tend to lie down for long periods and when

141

standing will hold all four feet close together. If only the front feet are affected, the hind feet will be placed under the body to take the weight off of the front hoofs. The front hoofs will be placed forward with the weight on the heels. The blood vessels will be full and pulsing over the fetlock, and the horse will show his anxiety by trembling, fast breathing, and high temperature. Indications of grain founder may not appear for twelve to eighteen hours after eating, and should not be expected too soon.

When first starting to move the horse will be slightly stiff and careful about placing his feet. At the first indication of the possibility of founder, stop working the horse, keep him warm, massage his legs and body, bed him down well, and feed him lightly. Remove the cause if it is apparent. Be sure to call the veterinarian. His treatment may include a diuretic, a purgative, antihistimines, intramuscular blood, "Normal Horse Serum," and dextrose.

If the condition is allowed to become chronic, changes in the hoof will occur. Because of the inflammation and increased blood supply, the hoof will grow faster and tend to curl up at the toe. As pressure separates the laminae, the coffin bone will no longer be supported, and the tip will rotate downward until, in extreme cases, it may push out through the sole. The horse will try to walk on this heels to avoid concussion to the bottom of the foot. The sole will drop, and the wall will develop rings from inflammation at the coronet.

Treatment must be started as soon as possible, and a veterinarian should always be called. Soak the feet with cold packs or tie the horse in a cool stream, keeping his body warm with a blanket. Give him warm water to drink. Cold compresses or water will help relieve pain, reduce the temperature, maintain vitality of the soft tissues, tone up the blood vessels, diminish the supply of blood, and limit exudation.

When preparing the foot for the shoe, lower the heels as much as possible. This balances the foot and takes the weight off the toe. Lowering the heels also puts more strain on the deep flexor tendon, which is already pulling on the coffin bone. This tendon glides over the navicular bone and then attaches to the underside of the coffin bone near the back end. Perhaps the additional strain helps to pull the back down, thus rotating the front end upward. The main factor in correcting founder is relieving the weight on the toe. Dub off the toe from the front of the hoof to make a more normal-looking foot. Don't worry about hitting the coffin bone as the point has rotated downward and will be out of the way. Remember this when lowering the heels. Keeping the foot flat, trim as much off of the heels as possible without injuring the point of the coffin bone. Trim the sole until it gives slightly, but be very careful about the coffin bone. Lowering the heels helps to rotate the coffin bone back to a more normal position. If the hoof is kept trimmed as described, many horses can be returned to usefulness in a year or so. This will depend largely on complications and side effects such as sidebone development, infection, etc. Trim the foot every three or four weeks to counteract the rapid growth produced by increased circulation.

Once the heels are trimmed and the wall leveled, lower the wall at the toe so that it does not come in contact with the shoe. With no weight on the toe, the wall and sole will be able to grow back together. In an extreme case, it may be necessary to remove all of the wall at the toe and most of the white line, which has been filled in with broken-down horn cells. This is no problem as the toe should not support any of the horse's weight.

A handmade shoe that has a wide web to protect the sole and is well-seated-out so that the sole does not rest on the shoe is best. If you cannot make a shoe, you may be able to weld a piece of one-eighth-inch metal around the inside edge of a keg shoe. Keep it an eighth of an inch from the bearing surface so that it will not put pressure on the sole when nailed on the hoof. A handmade shoe that is slightly thicker at the toe than at the heels will help rotate the coffin bone. Another method is to weld a bar across the shoe about one and one-half inches from the toe. This also makes the foot break over easily.

Every case must be dealt with individually. If the horse has a flat foot with a large frog, he could suffer from overexpansion and the frog must be trimmed or a thicker heel would be needed to lift the frog off the ground, thus reducing expansion.

A little gentle shoe pressure on the sole may help to support and flatten it. Use the smallest nail possible as the horn is generally of poor quality and large holes would make it more subject to cracking and drying. On poor-quality horn, side clips but not toe clips may be used. A bar shoe over a leather pad packed with pine

144

tar and oakum, is best for a horse with an extremely tender sole and a small frog. See that the hoofs contain the proper amount of moisture during the treatment.

HOOF PUNCTURES

The sole and frog can easily be punctured by nails, glass, and other sharp objects, or by "pricking" when the horse is shod. Any puncture should be considered serious and treated accordingly. The nearer the wound is to the center of the foot the more likely it is that there will be complications. Since tetanus bacteria are common in horse manure, the horse should be given a shot of tetanus antitoxin when injured. The horse should be vaccinated against tetanus and given a routine booster shot each year as normal procedure.

If the horse has been pricked while being shod, lameness may not become apparent for a day or two. If you suspect this has happened, pull the shoe. If the horse has been pricked, the offending nail will be wet and blue. When the actual wound is located, a syringe can be used to force a disinfectant into the hole.

Since a simple puncture can ruin a good horse, I cannot overemphasize the importance of a careful examination the moment the horse goes lame. Often the horse may limp a few steps and then appear sound only to have pus draining from the coronet a few days later. The wound may also bleed at first, making it easier to find. Each time a horse's feet are routinely cleaned, listen for the sound of the pick striking metal. When a foreign object is found, it should be removed and the wound treated immediately.

145

The objective in treatment is to prevent infection if possible, and if not, to make the pus drain through the wound in the sole rather than through the coronet, which is the path of least resistance. The hoof should be washed with soap and water and treated with a disinfectant. For new wounds the hole should be pared out, disinfected, and kept clean. The horse should be rested until healing occurs. If pus is already present, enlarge the wound (cut a good, deep funnel-shaped hole) and soak the hoof in one and one-half to two inches of warm water saturated with Epsom salts or with medication recommended by the veterinarian. Be sure the water does not cover the foot, as water will soften the coronet and increase the chances of the pus draining upward instead of down through the sole as desired. A rubber tub is handy for soaking a foot, and the horse may be left in it night and and day as needed. X rays will locate most of hard-to-find objects except wood or other soft materials.

Once pus has come to a head and drainage has stopped, the horse may be shod; but do not drive nails near the wound. Use a leather pad packed with pine tar and oakum if the sole needs protection; the pine tar acts as a germicide. If the wound needs both treatment and protection, trace the outline of the foot on a piece of sheet metal. Make the pattern small enough to fit under the shoe but inside the nail holes. Leave a tab at the front of the toe and one at the rear of each heel. Cut out this shape, tap it under the shoe, and bend up the tabs. The plate can be pulled out when treatment is required. Corns can also be treated using the same methods.

Navicular

Navicular disease is a fairly common chronic inflammation of the navicular bone, which lies beneath the middle third of the frog. It is one of the most important causes of lameness in horses and generally occurs in the front feet, although the hind feet can also be affected. Thoroughbred horses seem to be prone to navicular problems, and, directly or indirectly, it could be hereditary, although many cases are the result of injury. Poor nutrition is a contributing factor because a brittle bone will chip or break more easily. Concussion and puncture wounds that leave a "dry joint" inside the hoof are often involved, and sometimes the bone is broken or cracked.

A horse that has a navicular inflammation takes short, "stilty" steps, and may stumble often. Such movement becomes worse as the horse goes downhill; he may, however, warm out of it when the disease is in the initial stages, or lameness may be intermittent. The toe strikes the ground first, producing rapid wear, and may throw dirt upward. At rest the horse will point the foot. The horse may press his weight down on the heels to deaden the pain. The shoe will show no polishing under the heels from expansion as would a normal foot. Usually only one forefoot is affected, but should both forefeet become involved, the disease will probably be chronic in the first hoof before any symptoms appear in the second.

Sweeny (wasting away of the muscles) may be present in old cases and thrush (see later reference) may accompany the disease. The frog will shrink from lack of

147

use and the heels will grow higher and start to contract. As the frog becomes hard and unyielding, it no longer cushions the bone, and the concussion sets up inflammation, thus aggravating the situation.

The horse will show pain if the hoof testers are applied around the middle of the frog. Use the testers to check the ends of the bone by putting pressure on each side of the hoof. A veterinarian may listen with a stethoscope for internal noise as the hoof is flexed, since many cases are not advanced enough to show up on an X ray.

When shoeing the horse, the object is to prevent contraction and put some weight on the heels without discomfort to the horse. Shorten the toe of the hoof and roll the toe of the shoe to help the horse's stride. Make the shoe thin at the toe (one-quarter inch) and thick at the heels (three-quarters inch). Make the heels wide, beveling them slightly toward the outside to aid expansion, prevent contraction, and take some pressure off the bone. If a bar shoe is used, place the bar as far back as possible so that it does not put pressure over the bone itself. A "heart-bar" shoe gives the greatest protection, but don't let it rest too heavily on the frog. Do not use calks. A leather or rubber pad will help relieve pain and allow the horse to work.

As a last resort, a veterinarian may cut the nerves of the foot so that the horse can be used. This will generally prolong useful life a few years; however, it is dangerous, as the horse may injure his foot or get an infection, but show no signs of lameness. Later the foot may shrink or slough, depending on which nerves are cut, and the horse would no longer be safe to use.

148

QUITTOR

Quittor is an infection inside the hoof, generally involving the lateral cartilage. As pus forms it takes the route of least resistance and discharges at the top of the coronet.

It may be caused by a bruise or injury to the sensitive laminae or lateral cartilage. Sole punctures, tread wounds, infected corns, and wire cuts are common causes. A nail that is driven close to the sensitive tissues but does not penetrate will put pressure on this area and also cause injury. The problem is most prevalent in the forefeet and may be suspected if swelling, heat, and pain occur at the top of the hoof.

This is one of the most painful diseases a horse can have, and it can be relieved by draining the pus. Lined sinus tracts are formed which tend to heal from the top, breaking open again as the pus builds up and creates pressure. When the pus has been released, the horse will show much less lameness. The pus pocket can be located using a hoof tester or tapping lightly on the wall with a hammer. If the development is in the initial stages, an incision may be made through the sole and up along the wall to drain the pus. If the infection remains untended, an operation will have to be performed to remove all dead tissue and induce healing of the tracts. If the coronary band is cut in the process, the horn-producing cells will be destroyed and the hoof will always be defective. Some veterinarians now perform this operation by making an eliptical cut above the coronary band. In some early cases the dead tissue can be re-

149

moved by irrigating it with a 20 per cent silver nitrate solution, followed in ten minutes by a saline injection to neutralize the silver nitrate. These injections should be given daily until all necrotic (dead) tissue has been removed. An enzyme such as trypsin is then applied, thus aiding the removal of any other necrotic tissue that may develop.

The area should be shaved and kept bandaged to prevent contamination.

RINGBONE

Ringbone is a bony growth in the pastern area, and is divided into two categories—high and low. High ringbone, sometimes called an "osselet," occurs on the long pastern bone or on the upper part of the short pastern bone. Low ringbone occurs on the lower end of the short pastern bone and/or its joint with the coffin bone. High ringbone is generally less serious because it is less likely to affect the bone surfaces of the joint or the tendons. A ringbone may form anywhere on the pasterns; however, it is usually more serious if it occurs on the front or back of the pasterns than on the sides, since this is where the tendons are located. There are two kinds of ringbone—that which involves the joint surfaces and that which does not. If the bony growth does not involve the joints or tendons, no lameness may be present except during formation.

Ringbone is more common in the front feet than in the hind feet and often occurs in both front feet at the same time. When this happens the horse will point one front foot and then the other.

The tendency to develop ringbone is hereditary. A horse with an upright pastern does not dissipate the shock of concussion as well as a horse with a normal-sloping pastern. Conversely, a long-sloping pastern puts more strain on the bone structures, especially at the rear of the pastern. Horses that toe-in are predisposed to ringbone on the outside of the pasterns, while horses that toe-out are predisposed to ringbone on the inside. Trimming the foot out of balance will put strain on the tendons in the same way. Most ringbones are caused by injury, either directly to the pastern bones or by strain or sprain that sets up inflammation of the bone covering.

The object in shoeing is to relax the tendons at the points where they pass over the rough bony growths. In some cases the deposits may be removed surgically. The location of the growth is the key to the type of shoe to be used. If in front, use a thin-heeled shoe; if anywhere other than the front, use swelled heels. Some cases respond best to a full roller shoe that has both toe and heels thinned. Rocking the toe of the shoe will aid in removing some of the action from the affected joint. This is especially true if the joint grows together, and sometimes this is the only hope. If this fusion is necessary, the veterinarian will probably put the foot in a cast until the joint grows together. If the disease can be treated when it is first developing, the chances for retaining a usable horse are much better. X-ray methods are very useful since the horse becomes lame before the enlargement is apparent and, if the ringbone is inside the joint, are the only accurate way to diagnose the disease.

151

SEEDY TOE

Seedy toe is the destruction of the white line, or a "dry rot." A cavity forms which is usually filled with dirt and grit. It can occur anywhere in the white line, not necessarily at the toe as the name implies; however, the laminae are longer at the toe and more subject to change.

Seedy toe is the result of the same process that occurs in a foundered foot, only in a modified degree. Anything that inflames the sensitive laminae can be the cause— blows against the wall, nail wounds, and hard use of an unshod horse. When inflammation occurs, the increased blood supply causes pressure and separation of the laminae. Fluid is deposited and later the area fills with broken-down horn cells. In some cases the white line seems merely to separate from the wall, making an inward bend. (See "Tumors and Cankers of the Horn" later in this chapter.)

The cavity must be cleaned out and filled with pine tar and oakum before shoeing. When the horse is lame and the cavity is too deep to clean, it may be necessary to remove the detached wall by first rasping it until it is very thin and then cutting until every particle of the loose wall is removed. This area should be cleaned, covered with pine tar and oakum, bandaged, and covered with regular roofing tar.

You should lower the wall over the area before shoeing. You can also seat out the section of the shoe that goes over the affected wall to make sure there is no pressure on the hoof. This can be done with a grinder if heat is not available. Nails should be driven no closer than one inch to the cavity and no clip should come in contact with it.

SESAMOIDITIS

The tendons glide over the sesamoid bones, which act as a support, giving the tendons leverage. In this respect, these bones are the same as the navicular bone. They are located at the rear of the leg, making up the bulk of the fetlock. Any unusual strain on the ligaments attached to these bones can start the inflammation that leads to calcification and new bone growth. Horses with long toes and low heels are especially susceptible to this type of problem.

When the inflammation first appears, excessive synovial fluid is secreted and a windgall (see later refence) usually forms. As this continues, the fluid is replaced by fibrous tissue and bony deposits. An X ray may be taken after about three weeks to see if bony changes are occurring. If not, the lameness may be due to tendovaginitis, fracture of the bones, or injury to the suspensory ligament.

The horse should be rested and an effort made to reduce the inflammation. Alternating hot and cold packs as well as antiphlogistic packs will do this if treatment is started early. The veterinarian may then place the limb in a cast to allow healing without aggravation caused by movement.

When shoeing, lower the toe as much as possible and roll the toe of the shoe. Use a thick-heeled shoe or swelled heels to relieve the strain on the sesamoids.

SIDEBONES

Sidebones develop when the lateral cartilage of the coffin bone ossifies. Concussion, cracks, or injury cause the inflammation with its eventual bony deposits. Sidebones usually occur in the front feet and may affect one or both cartilages. If only one is involved, it is usually the outside cartilage. Sidebones are more common in the heavy draft breeds. Horses with upright pasterns, straight-walled feet, thick heels, and toe-in and toe-out stance are predisposed to this affliction. (If the toe points outward, suspect the inside cartilage and vice versa.) A foot trimmed out of balance can be a contributing factor because of the increased concussion on the high side.

Since hardening starts at the coffin bone and works up, you cannot feel it at first. Examine the leg with the weight on and off of the hoof. Heat and pain will be present during the ossification period, but when the hoof has altered its shape to fit the enlargement, pain usually stops.

In addition, as the cartilages lose their elasticity and expansion stops, the venous blood is not pumped from the foot, and the lower limb may swell. However, a small, unhealthy frog, contracted heels, or lack of exercise may also produce this effect.

The horse will point the foot while resting, and the toe will strike the ground before the heels when walking. Authors on the subject disagree as to which side grows high. The affected side may be lower than the sound side. This is opposite from what one would expect, as

154

usually, if part of the hoof is sore, the horse will try to avoid walking on it, and it will grow high through lack of wear. It is possible that the horse is trying to deaden the pain when he treads heavily on the affected side. Another theory is that, as the wall bulges outward, it has to shorten, and also becomes thinner and more subject to wear. I think that, if the horse is compelled to walk on the affected side, the new shoe should conform to this wear and the branch should be thinned. An unshod horse will have worn the hoof off to the least painful angle, so don't try to change it. You may want to lower the wall under the cartilage to reduce concussion.

To aid recovery, rest the horse and apply cold packs for several days to help relieve fever. If the feet are dry and hard, soak them until they become soft and moist. This will help to relieve the pain because the horn will yield, easing the internal pressure.

The toe of the shoe should be rocked, and the outer edge of the ground surface of the branch under the affected side should be rounded to help the foot roll over that side slightly. A handmade shoe is best. If you thin the branch, make it cover a wide area. Punch the nail holes a little closer to the edge than normal because of the thinned wall and keep the holes ahead of the quarter.

Since the foot can no longer expand normally, frog pressure is not required, and it could do harm by pressing the sensitive tissues against the unyielding cartilage. A thick felt or leather pad will help the horse by reducing concussion. A bar shoe will hold the pad, and

155

is necessary if the cartilages on both sides are affected.

In extreme cases, the wall can be cut through almost to the sensitive tissue so that it can expand and relieve internal pressure. A special tool is available for this operation, or a saw may be used. Three to seven cuts may be made parallel to the fibers, that is, from the ground to the coronet, but be careful not to injure the coronet. The same effect can be obtained by rasping the wall thin over the area. If these measures are taken, the foot must then be soaked and a dressing applied to keep it soft and to avoid any evaporation of the moisture it already contains.

SPLINTS

Splints are bony enlargements which usually appear on the inside of the front cannon bones. They rarely occur on the outside of the front legs or the hind legs. Splints are common, may or may not be serious, depending on their location, and can cause lameness during their formation. They detract from the appearance of the horse, and thus from the value, as do all other enlargements of this sort.

Splints are classed as high and low. A low splint is located down on the cannon bone and is harmless after formation has stopped; a high splint is located up toward the joint and is harmful to the degree that it interferes with the knee joint. If it interferes with the articular surfaces of the bones or the ligaments, it can cause permanent lameness.

Splints are a disease of young horses and are associated with hard training, poor conformation, incorrect shoeing, malnutrition, and injury. Fracture of the splint bone may be mistaken for an ordinary splint; however, the swelling is more diffuse and may extend the entire length of the splint bone. In most horses, a small swelling may be felt at the lower third of the cannon bone, but this is the natural enlargement at the lower end of the splint bone.

In this disease, as in most bone problems, lameness occurs before any swelling is apparent. Although the swelling may be slight, there will be heat and the area will be tender. The lameness may be intermittent, but it increases as the animal is exercised. This reaction is opposite to that of bone spavin, ringbone, navicular, and stringhalt. If the knee joint is involved, it becomes aggravated with use, and the horse will swing his leg outward from the knee to relieve the pain.

In some cases the splint does not behave normally but becomes larger and affects the rear of the cannon bone also. This is called a "pegged splint" and is much more serious, since it interferes with the suspensory ligament, causing permanent irritation and lameness.

To understand the development of splints, it is neccessary to have a simple understanding of the leg conformation. It is a simple matter to tell if a cannon bone is front or rear, left or right. The bone from a front leg is much flatter from front to back than that of a hind leg. Also, and this is what we are concerned with here, the inside of the bone is highest where it fits into the knee joint. Since the inside is higher, it takes more shock. This is why most splints occur on the inside. The splint bones themselves are apparently what is left of the

157

other toes as the horse evolved into a single-toed animal. In the young horse these bones are attached to the cannon bone by ligamentous tissue only. As the horse grows older, ossification occurs, and the bones are permanently attached; therefore a splint rarely occurs in an older horse.

If these bones or ligaments in a young horse are disturbed by one of the causes listed previously, an irritation is created in the periosteum (bone covering), causing inflammation and the resulting deposits of new bone.

Here is a test for splint lameness which has been used with varying degrees of success: Bend the leg at the knee like a jackknife and hold it in this position for a full minute, then start the horse quickly. If he has no problem when walking the first few steps, a splint may be causing the lameness.

A veterinarian should be consulted concerning the method of treatment, which could be anything from simply painting with iodine to scraping, sawing, or chiseling off the growth, or even removing the complete splint bone. Usually, because of the comparative harmlessness of splints and the likelihood that any irritating treatment may excite the parts and cause renewed disease development, it is not advisable to treat the case with drastic measures unless the usefulness of the animal is impaired.

One method of treatment which is becoming more common is to inject the area with corticosteriod to reduce the inflammation and prevent further bone growth. This treatment must be accompanied by prolonged rest.

158

Apply a shoe with a rocked toe and swelled heels to ease the breaking over. The horse should, of course, be rested until the inflammation has stopped, and his training should be altered or delayed for a year to avoid recurrence. The horseshoer should take every precaution to guard against interference (see Chapter X), as the splint would become very painful if the horse should hit it, and the irritation would prevent healing.

As inflammation is reduced and the splint heals, it will become slightly smaller because the surface of the bone smooths over somewhat, and the swollen tissues involved are reduced. Rest, good care, and proper nutrition are important under any form of treatment.

The importance of splints may also reflect what is happening to other bones in the body. Perhaps the colt needs a change in both training and mineral diet.

STIFLED

The stifle joint is located between the hip and the hock and is the largest joint in the body. When the stifle becomes dislocated, the horse will hold his leg back rigidly, being unable to bring it forward. A dislocated stifle is also called luxation, slipping, or upward fixation of the patella. It can occur in any horse, but colts and horses with long straight legs are usually affected. Sometimes the leg will not lock, but the patella will click in and out with each step the horse takes. A young horse may outgrow this affliction.

Although it may occur naturally in young horses, in older horses it is caused by injury. A fall or a sudden start, with the legs slipping too far forward, can dislocate the joint. The horseshoer must keep this in mind when throwing a horse. A horse can be injured by tying the foot up behind, usually to the tail, and then falling on his stifle. It is safer either to throw the horse or to tie a ring in his tail, run the rope from the pastern through the ring, and have someone hold his foot up from behind so that it can be released if he falls. If you are alone and need to tie the hind leg back, tie it to his neck also (see the section "Tying Up a Hind Foot" in Chapter VI).

When the patella becomes dislocated, it must be slipped back in place as soon as possible so that the horse will not fall down and injure himself further. If someone is available to help you, put a rope around the pastern and have your helper draw the foot gently forward. You will feel a bulge on the outside of the stifle joint. Standing behind the horse, apply extreme pressure to the top and back of the bump, and it will go back into place with a "click." If you are alone, it will be necessary to use your foot and leg to push the affected leg forward, while pushing the patella back in place. Remember that the horse can kick again as soon as the joint is in place. Rub the stifle with strong mustard or liniment so the tissues will swell and help to keep the patella from slipping out again. Rest the horse in a level corral or pasture. Counterirritants will help to restore vitality.

If this dislocation happens very often, the joint may become chronically inflamed, and the veterinarian may perform a simple operation by cutting one of the liga-

160

ments before this happens. There are three ligaments holding the patella. The inside one is severed at its lower attachment. The horse should then be rested in a stall for a week and not used for six or eight weeks. The patella will not slip out again, and the horse will be usable; however, the limb will not be quite as strong as it was previously.

There is a special shoe that can be used immediately after the patella slips out the first time. It is nailed on the sound hoof and consists of an iron bar welded over the shoe so that it barely touches the pastern above the front of the hoof (see the accompanying illustration). This hurts the horse when he attempts to use the sound leg, forcing him to keep his weight on the unsound leg so that the patella will not slip out before it has a chance to heal. The same thing can be accomplished by shoeing the sound foot with heel calks that are two or three

STIFLE SHOE

Top view   *Side View*

161

inches high. This shoe should not be left on any longer than necessary, as it strains the sound leg. Of course, the horse cannot be used while shod with either of these shoes.

STRAINS AND SPRAINS

A sprain is the tearing or yielding of any of the muscles, tendons, ligaments or the sheaths supporting them. A strain is simply excessive stretching. If the periosteum of the bone is involved, the area will become inflamed, resulting in bone deposition, and ringbone may develop. In a sprain the tendon will sometimes tear out a small piece of bone where it is attached. Sprains may accompany any of the tendon disorders or occur by themselves. A long pastern, weak conformation, or a foot that is too long makes the horse more susceptible to this sort of disorder.

Check for sprains with the horse's weight on the leg. New sprains are swollen and puffy, but older sprains may be hard and well defined to the touch.

If the suspensory ligament is involved, the swelling will be close to the bone, while if the flexor tendons are involved, the swelling will be closer to the back of the leg. Usually it is hard to distinguish the two.

If a sprain occurs while the horse is being used, immediately apply a tight bandage before moving him. Your shirt can be used if nothing better is available. Treat the area with cold water or cold packs as soon as possible, and then continually for one or two days, depending on severity. This treatment will keep the swelling to a minimum. If the injury is not discovered for a day or two, use hot packs to reduce the swelling. An electric heating pad is good as it is thermostatically controlled and requires less attention than hot-water packs. If the strain is in an area where swelling is not a big problem, you may use hot applications immediately. Be sure to check with a veterinarian.

Further treatment consists of rest, counterirritants, and massage. Elastic- or rubber-support bandages should be used when the horse is returned to work after a prolonged rest. There is a plastic inflatable splint on the market, which, although it is generally used in fractures to immobilize and cushion the limb, can also be used for a sprain. A two-inch strip cut from a rubber inner tube will also work.

If a support or pressure bandage is used, check frequently to see that it is not too tight. Swelling, nonuse of the leg, and increased temperature indicate that the bandage is too tight.

An electric vibrator may be used for massage. Massage and counterirritants increase local circulation, thus relieving pain and swelling. Massage in a downward direction (same direction as the blood moves from the heart) and use the same pressure as you would on your own leg.

STRINGHALT

Since stringhalt cannot be corrected by shoeing, I mention it for general information only.

Stringhalt is the jerking of the hind leg while walking or trotting. It affects different horses differently and does not follow any set pattern. It generally is worse when a horse is turning, after resting, and during cold weather. The condition improves as the horse is exercised. Therefore, if you suspect stringhalt, let the horse cool off and then back him uphill. The condition will become more apparent if it exists.

The veterinarian will remove a tendon on the outside of the hock in order to treat this condition.

TENDON DISORDERS

Tendon afflictions such as strains or filled or bowed, lacerated, ruptured, or contracted tendons are common to the saddle horse. Among their causes are overexertion, injuries, strains, poor conformation, and improper shoeing. These same causes also affect the ligaments, which bind bone to bone while tendons bind muscles to bone.

Prompt attention to these conditions may return the horse to normal, but if treatment is postponed, the ailment will become chronic and the horse will be ruined. Any injury to the tendons or ligaments should be considered serious as these tissues are inelastic and when torn require a long time to heal. Healing is complicated by the horse's natural movements.

As many books and articles have already been written on the location and function of the tendons, only the points pertinent to horseshoeing will be discussed here. The horseshoer should know that there are flexor tendons, which draw the leg up, and extensor tendons, which extend the leg forward. He should also understand how the tendon sheaths lubricate and protect the tendons. He should understand that the suspensory ligament is primarily what keeps the horse from falling down when he goes to sleep. There are three types of ligaments: binding ligaments, which hold the bones together; capsular ligaments, which secrete and contain the synovial fluid; and check ligaments, which hold the tendons against the bones. Curb, which is a sprain of a hock ligament, is discussed earlier in this chapter under the heading "Curb." (It is interesting to note that there are no muscles below the knee.)

The longer and more sloping the pastern is, the greater the strain on the flexor and suspensory ligaments. (Horses with long, sloping pasterns provide a smooth ride.) More tendon injuries occur at the fetlock than in the upper leg where the tendons are more firmly combined, giving strength and assistance to each other. In any tendon trouble, it is a good idea to support the leg with bandages when the horse is being returned to work. If tendon injuries are not treated promptly, the tendons become thick and hardened and will not respond to treatment.

A very good rest shoe can be made for injured or sprained flexor tendons. First, fit the shoe to the foot and determine how much elevation is needed for the heels. Now take a piece of $\frac{1}{4}$-inch by $1\frac{1}{4}$-inch iron that is twice the height necessary to raise the heels plus the distance across the outside of the heels on the fitted shoe plus a one-inch allowance for bending and making the rest slightly wider than the branches. When you cut the stock, cut each end with about a 15° bevel, so that when it is bent and welded under the shoe, the rest will be flat on the ground. If you want the heels an inch high, measure an inch from each end and make right angle

165

bends. Weld this to the branches under the heels. This shoe gives good, wide support and will not sink in the ground unless it is extremely soft. The bottom of the toe is chamfered off so that both it and the rest will be flat on the ground and will not rock.

REST SHOE

Bowed Tendon

A bowed tendon exists when the synovial fluid and/or the tendon escapes through the tendon sheath and bulges out at the rear of the leg anywhere from the knee to the fetlock. Lameness accompanies the heat, swelling, and inflammation. This condition responds to treatment and rest; however, every effort must be made to avoid strain to the area or the bowed tendon will probably recur. This condition may be accompanied by ligament injury and fracture of the sesamoid bones.

Treatment consists of rest, counterirritants, massaging, and bandaging. A recommended compound is the combination of one-third iodine, one-third glycerine, and one-third carbolic acid. The hair is clipped, the compound is rubbed against the hair, and the leg is snugly bandaged for several days and then washed with Castile soap. When bandaging, be sure to place plenty of cotton around the leg first and then use an elastic bandage to

166

help support the tendon. Check the leg frequently to see that the bandage is not too tight. Counterirritants may be massaged into the area, and after exposing the leg to the air for about thirty minutes, it can be bandaged in the above manner. It is best to cross-tie the horse during this treatment so that he cannot chew the bandage and smear the medication.

A shoe with high heels will relax the tendon so that healing may start, but do not leave it on after healing is well under way. The tendon could contract or adhesions could develop between the relaxed tendon and the sheath, or even other tendons. A veterinarian may recommend corticosteriod injections, putting the leg in a cast, or surgical correction.

Filled Tendon

A filled tendon is basically the same as a "bowed tendon," although the tendon does not protrude through the sheath. Treatment is the same as for a bowed tendon.

Contracted Tendon

Contraction of the flexor tendons may be congenital or develop as a sequel to injury or disease. If congenital, it will affect both legs, usually the front ones, but if caused by an injury, it will affect one leg only.

A horse with a contracted tendon will knuckle forward at the knee and will stand and travel on the toe. This is often called "broken down" or "knee sprung." It is common in newborn colts, who generally outgrow it. Common causes are running the horse downhill and standing him in a stall with an inclined floor.

167

Horses with this condition are not safe to use, and a long-standing condition will probably not respond to treatment. A veterinarian should be consulted to find out whether a tenotomy, or cutting of the tendons, should be performed. A shoe with high heels helps to make the horse usable to a certain extent but does not help to correct the defect. It is a good idea to feed the horse from the floor instead of a manger.

Lacerated Tendon

Laceration of the tendons is common and often caused by wire cuts. If caused from internal strain, the skin will be intact. If the extensor tendons are cut, the horse will be unable to extend the toe. Extensor tendons have a better chance to heal than flexor tendons.

Generally no attempt is made to sew extensor tendons together; instead, the leg is put in a cast in its normal position. When the cast is removed, the foot is shod with a special shoe which keeps the toe extended so that the tendon can heal.

First, fit the shoe. Then weld on a three-inch toe extension and make a bar that conforms to the front of the cannon bone just above the pastern (see accompanying illustration). With the foot in the position desired, measure the distance from the bar to the toe extension and weld a brace from each side of the extension onto the bar. Since it is desirable to keep the shoe as light as possible, pipes may be used for these braces instead of iron bars. Nail the shoe to the foot, pad the leg and bar, and bind the bar to the leg with adhesive tape.

A soft piece of leather laced over the cotton will hold it in place and protect the leg from the bar. With this shoe in place the horse cannot flex his toe, and the tendon is given a chance to heal.

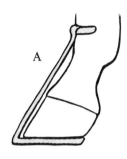 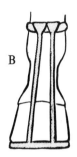

SHOE FOR IMMOBILIZING PASTERN AREA

Side view   *Front view*

Damage to the rear tendons may be determined by the position of the fetlock. If the outside flexor tendon is cut, the fetlock will drop but will not touch the ground. If both the outside and inside flexors are cut, the fetlock will drop and the toe will be in the air when the horse puts his weight on the leg. If both the flexors and the suspensory ligament are cut, the fetlock will rest on the ground. In the last case, the horse should be destroyed. In the other instances, the veterinarian will suture the tendons and place the leg in a cast with the fetlock flexed.

In some cases it may be decided not to use a cast

at all but to start with a special shoe. When this is to be done, make a shoe like the one described for severed extensor tendons, but fit the brace behind the leg instead of in front. If the horse is shod and the veterinarian does not think he should be subjected to reshoeing, the new shoe may be wired to the old one. It is generally best, however, to pull the old shoe.

When the cast is removed, the fetlock must be supported by a special shoe that is made as follows. A plate shoe is fitted to the hoof. An extension is then welded to each heel so that it comes a little past the rear of the fetlock when the foot is in a normal position. At this point, right-angle bends are made in the extensions to a point just above the bottom of the fetlock, where a right-angle bend is again made, bringing the extensions alongside the bottom of the fetlock. Now a leather strap is secured between the extensions so that the fetlock can rest on it and be supported. Once the dimensions of the extension have been determined for a particular horse, the shoe is easy to make. It must be made of iron that is strong enough that the horse's weight cannot bend it. Three-eighths-inch iron is about right for the average horse. This shoe should be used for three to six months, and then the horse should be shod with a shoe having two- or three-inch trailers on both branches. This shoe helps support the fetlock and prevents the heels from suddenly dropping into a hole and straining the tendons. If the stitches pull out, the ends will be boomed and new stitches will not hold well.

If either of these shoes is used on the front feet, the

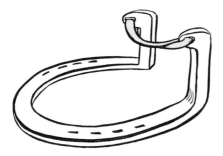

FETLOCK-SUPPORTING SHOE

horse can never be allowed to move at a fast gait; and if he is moved at all, his hind feet should be slowed by lowering the heel, making the shoe full at the toe and long at the heels so that he does not tread on the fore-shoe. If the shoe is to be used for a long period, it should be hard-surfaced.

THOROUGHPIN

A thoroughpin is a soft, puffy enlargement in the hollow of the hock between the shank bones and large tendon, called the hamstring. It can occur at the same time as, or even be connected to, a soft swelling on the inner front of the hock, known as a bog spavin. Both are caused by excess synovial fluid or "joint oil" described under "Windgall," discussed later in this chapter. A thoroughpin can usually be seen from both the inside and outside of the hock, but it is generally more prominent on the inside. The condition is most apparent when viewed from behind.

171

Thoroughpin is more serious than windgall because it causes heat, tenderness, and lameness. It is also often associated with poor conformation of the hock, which will disqualify the horse for hard work.

The horse should be rested and shod with high-heeled calks, at least five-eighths of an inch higher than the toe, to keep tendon pressure off of the hock as much as possible. In a handmade shoe, swelled heels are better than calks as there is less concussion. A good wide toe and heel calks turned out slightly will give lateral support to keep the leg from twisting. The same treatment can be used as for windgall, with the addition of special pressure pads and bandages.

THRUSH

Thrush is a common infection, although generally very mild. It occurs in the hollows between the frog and the sole and is easily recognized by the presence of a moist, black, bad-smelling discharge and heat in the bulbs of the heels.

Thrush results from unhygienic conditions and is therefore more common in stalled horses. It can also result from improper shoeing, such as using high-heeled calks which keep the frog off the ground and do not permit it to function normally. Horses with high heels and straight-walled feet are susceptible to thrush. It often accompanies other afflictions such as navicular disease and contracted heels. Thrush responds readily to early treatment, but if not checked, it can involve the sensitive tissues under the horny frog and sole and ruin the horse permanently.

172

Treatment consists first of removing the cause and placing the horse in hygienic surroundings. Stalls should be cleaned often and treated with lime, and the feet should be kept dry. Trim out all diseased tissue of the frog and sole and treat daily with a drying agent such as tincture of iodine or turpentine. If the sensitive tissues are involved, the iodine may be diluted with water. There are several good commercial medicines available, which are both germicidal and caustic, to remove dead tissues. Counterirritants applied to the heels will hasten the growth of new, sound horn. In extreme cases the foot may have to be poulticed for a few days in a leather boot. A veterinarian should look at the hoof and determine the necessary treatment.

Generally, removing the shoes and letting the horse run in a dry, clean pasture, while giving daily treatment, is sufficient. If the horse cannot be turned out and must be used, he should be shod with a low-heeled, three-quarter or bar shoe that will put pressure on the frog. Trim the heels of the frog so that a hoof pick can be used to keep the foot clean. Don't use a pad unless it is necessary, for a pad keeps air from the frog and allows filth to accumulate.

Tumors and Cankers of the Horn

A horn tumor occurs in the wall and results in a flattening of the outer wall and an indentation of the white line. It can be brought on by anything that causes inflammation of the horn-secreting tissues such as cracks, tread wounds, or blows.

Sometimes these injuries will cause a hole in the horn,

173

which then grows downward until it can be trimmed off, leaving a sound hoof. Use a flat shoe, do not drive nails through or near the tumor, and lower the wall below the tumor where it rests on the shoe.

A canker occurs in the sole and frog. It is much more common in large lymphatic horses with thick skins and flat feet and in horses with white feet. Unhygienic conditions and extreme moisture promote its development. Once it becomes chronic, it is difficult to heal, and the tissues bleed readily. When the infection follows an injury, a fetid, watery discharge develops, which undermines and destroys the surrounding horn. The living tissues are swollen and dark-colored and are covered with cheesy masses of fetid, partly dried horn matter. When there has been no injury, these symptoms occur in the clefts of the frog.

Treatment consists of removing all affected tissues, soaking for several hours in an astringent solution, shoeing with a plate shoe, and using a piece of sheet metal under the shoe that can be slipped in and out (see "Hoof Punctures" mentioned earlier). The foot is packed with oakum and treated with a commercially prepared caustic stimulating agent or a mixture of copper and zinc sulfate crystals. The packing should be changed frequently, and the foot should be wrapped in a sack or boot for protection and sanitation.

WINDGALL

Windgall, or wind puff as it is sometimes called, is the swelling of the sacs that make synovial fluid to lubricate the tendons or the swelling of the tendon sheaths themselves. In bad cases both may be involved. Lameness is usually not present initially.

Windgalls occur around the fetlock joints of all four feet. The same condition occurs at the hock and knee and is then called bog spavin, thoroughpin, or windgall, but horseshoeing treatment differs for each of these afflictions.

A windgall is firm when the horse is standing on the leg and soft when the foot is raised. Exercise will usually make it smaller, but it fills up again after resting. Windgall can result from anything that strains the tendons, such as fast starts, slipping, or extremely heavy loads. It can also occur from external injury, such as being kicked by other horses.

Windgall will respond to early treatment before inflammation develops and the horse becomes lame. A valuable horse should be rested for several months after the irritation disappears or it will return. Of course, the cause should be determined and removed or remedied to prevent recurrence. If the horse is too young for the work he is doing, his training should be delayed. New cases should be treated continually during the day with cold water or ice packs alternated with water and snugly wrapped at night with an elastic bandage. Later, a counterirritant should be massaged into the area and a snug bandage applied. This treatment will cause the excess fluid to be absorbed and strengthen the walls of the sac. If the condition is not treated, the windgall may harden and cause lameness. If it has gone to this stage, a veterinarian should be consulted for possible surgical treatment or injections.

The horseshoer should make sure that the foot is perfectly balanced and level. The shoe should be removed, and the horse should be rested in a soft, level corral or pasture. When he is returned to work, use a light plate shoe. Do not use calks.

X.

Physical Disorders and Gait Defects

THE SKILLED FARRIER can control the position of the foot at rest and in flight, but corrective measures are usually an aid, not a cure. Special trimming and shoeing can make most horses usable, although a halt in corrective techniques may allow some reversion in mature horses. Horses with poor conformation are especially vulnerable to gait defects; if nature didn't do much for the horse, the farrier can't either. A colt's chances for permanent improvement are, however, much greater when regular corrective measures are applied.

A horse's natural gait is usually the best, so if the horse is getting along all right, he may not need special attention. In other instances, just a quarter-inch change on a corrective shoe can do a lot. Two horses with the same fault, however, may require different shoeing techniques. If the results are uncertain, put a bell boot on the opposite foot until you can be sure the horse will not injure himself. Sometimes a special shoe is effective in confirming or altering the gait only at fast speeds.

THE COMPLETE HORSESHOEING GUIDE

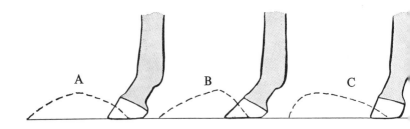

PATH OF FLIGHT AS AFFECTED BY HOOF ANGLE

Average foot makes a perfect arc.	*Sloping foot is slow to break over, rises highest in the first half of the stride, and has a longer stride.*	*Stumpy foot breaks over quickly and is highest during the last half of the stride.*

BASE-NARROW

In a base-narrow horse the feet will be inside a pair of perpendicular lines drawn from the center of each limb at the chest as shown in the accompanying illustration. Often these horses are also pigeon-toed, and the foot lands on the outside of the hoof, wearing this area down. A base-narrow condition in the hind legs is often accompanied by bowlegs. Base-narrow, pigeon-toed, and

178

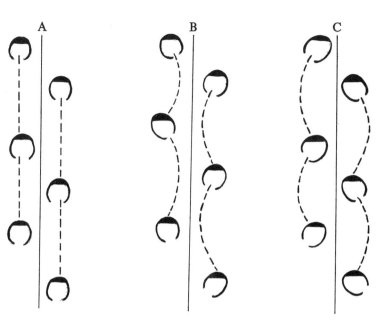

PATH OF FLIGHT AS AFFECTED BY CROOKED FEET
(*The shaded area shows where the foot will break over.*)

Normal	*Base-wide, toe-wide, splayfooted*	*Base-narrow, toe-narrow, pigeon-toed*

broken-out problems cause a tendency to "paddle" (see reference later in this chapter) because the foot breaks over the outside. If the horse is base-narrow and his toes

179

point straight ahead or out, he will have a tendency to interfere. This is not common.

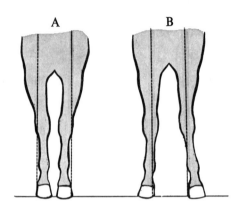

CONFORMATION DEFECTS I

Base-narrow   *Base-wide*

When trimming the hoofs of the affected feet, lower the inside walls as much as possible, and after several shoeings the feet should be straight. An outside trailer on the shoes of the affected feet will be helpful, and a lateral extension on the outside toes, acting as levers to turn the feet, will cause the hoofs to break over straight. Other methods include welding a bar diagonally across the break-over point, thinning the toe of the shoe where the foot should break over, using a half-shoe on the low side only, and welding one-quarter-inch rod around

180

the bottom of each branch, but not at the toe, encouraging the foot to break over the toe.

Rarely does a hoof toe-in and remain high on the outside, or vice versa. Normal corrective measures would aggravate the situation. Instead, balance the foot and fit the shoe as closely as possible to the inside of the toe.

Base-Wide and Splayfooted

Base-wide feet are outside a pair of perpendicular lines drawn from the center of each limb at the chest. A base-wide condition is more serious than a base-narrow one as there is greater chance of interference. This is because the foot breaks over the inside of the toe and therefore tends to have an inward arc of flight. Base-wide is less common in the hind legs, but if it occurs here, the horse is more likely to interfere than if it occurs in the forelegs.

Lower the hoof on the outside as much as possible and fit the shoe as closely as possible to the outside, letting the white line be the guide. Fit the shoe full on the inside, especially at the toe. If the condition is severe, add a lateral extension to the inside of the toe to make the foot break over the toe and fly straight.

The same method is used to correct the splayfooted condition except that a swelled heel is added on the inside branch. This problem is more serious than a simple base-wide condition as often the inside quarters and heels are also contracted. If the colt is young (less than three years old), it is possible to straighten the pastern and spread the heels, but an older horse will have to

181

wear a corrective shoe for the rest of his life. A shoe with a thickened inside branch will help to straighten the pastern.

Thoroughbred and Quarter Horses seem to be predisposed to this condition. The outer wall is more slanting and longer and thicker than the inner wall. The outer quarters are curved more than the inner quarters, and the weight falls largely on the inner half of the hoof.

The methods of treatment as described under "Base-Narrow" apply if used in reverse; for example, when it says to lower the inside wall, lower the outside wall for a base-wide horse, etc.

COW-HOCKED AND BOWLEGGED

When the horse's hocks are close together, the legs are cow-hocked, and the horse will probably be base-wide (see the accompanying illustration). When coming to a sliding stop, the feet will slide far apart unless a corrective shoe is applied. (See "Rodeo Horses" in Chapter XI.) This is a serious defect for a working horse as strain is thrown on the inside of the hock and could cause bone spavin.

Since the feet tend to break over on the worn inside area, the horse's hoofs will fly inward and may interfere. A common method of shoeing is to use a lateral extension on the inside toe and a swelled heel on the inside branch. Another method is to use a short inside trailer, sometimes with a calk under it. The object here is to brake the inside of the hoof, rotating the toe inward as the foot lands so that the hoof will break over the

182

center of the toe. A projection on the inside is dangerous, however, and while it is being used, the opposite leg should be wrapped and a bell boot applied for protection. An outside trailer may help some horses, and this method could be tried, reversing the shoes after they are fitted. The theory here is that the trailer will hit first and "flop" the foot inward just as it lands.

The inside wall of the hind feet of a young colt with this condition will be low; therefore, when trimming the

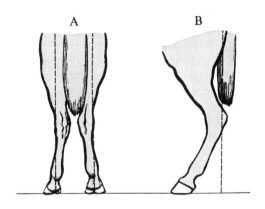

CONFORMATION DEFECTS II

Cow-hocked—Hocks are inside perpendicular lines.   *Sickle-hocked—Leg is forward of perpendicular line.*

These are both serious defects for a working horse because they cause excess strain at the hock, which could lead to disease or an early breakdown of the horse.

183

hoofs, do not touch the inside at all, but start at the center of the toe, taking as much off the outside wall from toe to heel as possible. The inside branch of the shoe can be thickened or leather shims can be used under the shoe. This procedure will help to straighten the feet and legs, or at least keep them from becoming worse.

The opposite of cow-hocked is bowlegged. If a horse is bowlegged, he will be base-narrow, his feet will fly outward, and his heels may twist outward just as the foot starts to break over. In this case use a square-toed shoe with a trailer on the outside branch that is turned out at a 45° angle and has a calk under it.

CROSS-FIRING

Cross-firing is the striking of the forefoot and opposite hind foot. Pacers are about the only horses troubled by it. A horse that toes-out in front and toes-in in back has the worst problem. Anything can be used that will correct foot alignment and provide a straight and true stride.

If the horse is toe-wide in front, use a grab or extension on the inside of the shoe to encourage the foot to break over the center of the toe. Bevel the outside branch to delay its contact with the ground and extend the inside branch three-eighths of an inch beyond the heel. Round the outer edge of the ground surface on the inside branch so that, if striking does occur, it will not damage the hind foot too much.

If the horse is toe-narrow in back, use a trailer on the outside branch and cut the inner branch a little short, thinning it from toe to heel. A lateral extension on the outside will also help. Many times pacers wear protective pads.

Flat Feet and Overexpansion

Horses with large, flat feet may suffer from overexpansion of the hoof when it contains a lot of moisture, which makes it more flexible. This is especially true of weak-heeled horses that have soft walls from the quarters back or horses with heel injuries. In these cases a bar shoe and leather pad may be necessary. Overly large feet will slow the horse down and decrease his agility. These feet should be trimmed as small as possible. Using the white line as a guide, leave enough wall to support the horse's weight and hold the shoe.

In extreme cases side clips or fine nail holes punched in the heels will retard expansion. The object is to reduce the expansion and the resulting friction, which previously had kept the heels worn down against the shoe. The frog can be trimmed or kept off the ground with thickened heels, and the branches may be beveled to the inside if necessary. If too much moisture or gumbo soils are part of the problem, keep the horse in a drier place.

Forging and Overreaching

Forging occurs when the horse's hind feet hit the front feet or shoes. Some horses strike the inner edge of the foot, some the outer edge, and some the bottom of the front shoe. It is necessary to find out where the foot is striking before a cure can be prescribed. Chalk the hind

185

foot around its edges, work the horse, and then examine the front feet for chalk marks.

Some horses like to hear the clicking noise made when the shoes hit each other, and will forge just to hear the noise. In this case the wall may be left protruding over the hind shoe, thus deadening the sound.

A colt that is not confirmed in his gaits may forge after he is shod, even though he didn't before, simply because of the increased weight. If the horse strikes the inside of the front shoe, beveling the inside edges may help. The heels of the front shoe should always be short so that the toe of the hind shoe does not catch them and tear the shoe off.

Horses with long legs and short backs tend to forge. This is true of Arabians. Setting the saddle too far back or riding on the cantle may also make the horse forge. Other causes are a long toe in front, front foot angle "broken back," corresponding feet not of the same size, hind feet shod too long at the toe, heels left too high, or fatigue.

Several methods are used to correct this defect. Sometimes using a heavier shoe in front may increase the length of the stride enough so that the feet will clear.

Often it is assumed that the hind toe should be shortened if the hind foot hits the front one. This is generally not true, as lowering and shortening the toe will make the hind foot break over faster and intensify the problem.

The most general method used is to quicken the front feet and delay the hind ones. To do this, the toes of the front feet are shortened, and the shoes are made with rocked toes and swelled heels. The heels of the hind feet are lowered as much as possible (don't change the natural angle more than 3°), and the branches are left long and extended straight back or slightly outward. A toe calk or thickened toe may also be used.

Using very light shoes, both in front and back, and rocking the toes is a second shoeing correction. Heel calks should be added on hind shoes. The rocked toes make the horse pick up his feet quicker and higher, thus shortening the stride.

A third method is to rock the toe of the front shoe, square the toe of the hind shoe, and make the hind shoe branches long and half the thickness of the toe.

Any of these methods, or a combination, may have to be used. Occasionally a very short-bodied horse cannot be corrected by special shoeing. A drastic measure that is then used is to weld a piece of iron about a half an inch thick across the heels of the front shoes and the toe of the hind ones.

Overreaching is basically the same as forging except that the horse catches the bulbs of the heels on the front feet. Corrections are the same as for forging, but in this case the horse may wear bell boots for protection. In addition, the inner border of the toe of the hind shoe is rounded so that it will not cut. Occasionally a horse will have a wound on his hind foot similar to an over-reach wound. This may be caused by other horses crowding from behind.

Interfering and Speedy Cutting

Interfering happens when one foot hits the opposite

foot or leg, and it is more common in the hind legs. It is called speedy cutting when the leg is hit above the fetlock.

A few of the many causes are heavy shoes (especially on young horses), fatigue, shoes too full on the inside or too pointed at the toe (not giving the foot lateral support as it breaks over), and unbalanced feet. Defects in conformation, such as a narrow chest, legs set too close together, cow-hocked legs, toe-out feet, base-wide position, or foot broken-in, make a horse susceptible to interfering. The causes can be either temporary or permanent.

When the injury occurs, the horse may carry the leg a few steps and then show lameness, but he will get over it quickly unless it happens again.

Generally, if the pastern or foot is crooked, it is necessary to lower the outside wall before anything else is done. Remove flares from the inside of the feet. The feet may be chalked to determine where the foot hits; however this usually is not necessary since the hair on the opposite leg will be roughened or an actual cut or sore will be present. Use a light plate shoe when possible and always round the outer edge of the inside branch so that it will not do too much damage if it does hit. A "drop-crease" or "feather-edged" shoe with a thin inner branch can be made. This thin branch is set in as far as possible while still enabling the shoer to get some nails in the white line.

PADDLING

Paddling is the act of swinging the foot in an outward

188

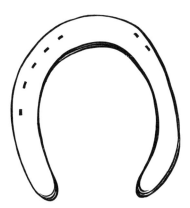

FEATHEREDGED SHOE

arc and is not as serious as an inward arc since the opposite leg is not injured in the process. If the motion doesn't seem to cause problems, it may be better not to try to correct it, especially in young horses, if it can't be cured by trimming. There are many causes of paddling. A long-backed horse is more likely to develop a swing to his gait than a short-backed horse. It is said that working the horse on a tight longe line will encourage the habit. A base-narrow and a toe-narrow (pigeon-toed or toed-in) horse will paddle because the foot will break over the outside of the toe, starting the foot on its outward arc. Also, a horse with a foot in a broken-out position will paddle.

If any of these conditions exist (see chart on "Conformation Defects" at the end of this chapter), lower the inside wall before doing anything else. Use a shoe with lateral extension on the outside of the toe and a slightly squared toe. Use as light a shoe as possible. Lowering the heels will cause the foot to travel closer to the ground, thus reducing the lateral swing. Leaving the wall longer at the toe will have the same effect as lowering the heels. Do not use a rolled toe or heel calks, for they increase the height of the arc.

Scalping

Scalping occurs when the hind fetlock comes in under the front foot and hits the toe. To prevent this, make the front foot raise quicker by rocking and shortening the toe. Swelled heels may also be used if necessary.

Sickle-Hocked

A sickle-hocked horse is one that has his hind legs set under his body, forward of a perpendicular line from his hip (see the illustration "Conformation Defects II" earlier in this chapter). If the toe is too high, lowering it will move the legs back. In contrast, a horse with his legs set behind the line is said to be "camped behind." Lowering the heels will move the legs forward if the heels are too high.

The sickle-hocked defect in conformation makes the horse susceptible to lameness, especially of the hock.

A horse that is slightly sickle-hocked can be taught a sliding stop with less trouble, but the legs will probably break down under heavy use.

Stumbling

There are many things that will make a horse stumble,

but in general, any time the toe touches the ground before the heels do, the horse is liable to stumble. The main causes are listed below.

Temporary

1. Calks, especially toe calks
2. Heels too high
3. Heavy shoes
4. Fatigue
5. Shoes fitted too full at the toe
6. Shoes too pointed at the toe
7. Wall at the toe too long
8. Undeveloped muscles

Permanent

1. Stumpy shoulders and pasterns
2. Narrow chest
3. Weak front legs
4. Front legs set too far back and not perpendicular
5. Opposite feet not the same size
6. Neck and head not properly set on shoulders
7. Stilty action or attempting to land on the toe

Always use as light a shoe as possible. Shorten and rock the toe to ease breaking over, induce greater elevation of the hoof in flight, and reduce concussion and fatigue. Use a plate shoe but leave the heels as high as possible. If this is not effective, use heel calks to change the hoof angle so that the feet will be higher during the last half of the stride and make contact with the ground at a steeper angle.

Some horses are just naturally "three-gaited"—stum-

Conformation Defects of Forelegs

Defect	Cause	Effect on gait	Area under strain	Remarks	Horseshoer's correction
Base-wide	Leg	Wings in, may interfere	Inside of fetlock and pastern	Often splay-footed, feet are outside perpendicular lines drawn from center of each side of chest, inside of hoof shows wear	Lower outside wall, square toe, and put lateral extension on inside
Base-narrow	Leg	Paddles	Outside of fetlock and pastern	Often pigeon-toed, feet are inside perpendicular lines drawn from center of each limb at chest, outside of hoof shows wear	Lower inside wall, square toe and put lateral extension on outside
Feet broken in	Trimming	Interference	Inside pastern	Refers to hoof only (top of hoof bent in)	Lower outside wall
Feet broken out	Trimming	Paddles	Outside pastern	Refers to hoof only (top of hoof bent out)	Lower inside wall
Pigeon-toed (toe-narrow or toe in)	Whole leg or from fetlock down	Paddles	Outside pastern	Correct trimming of colts will prevent worsening of defect, hoof wears on out-side	Lower inside wall; watch for contraction, sidebones, and corns on outside heel; square toe; and put lateral extension on outside

Defect	Cause	Interference	Notes/Corrective measures
Splayfooted (toe-wide or toe-out)	Whole leg or from fetlock down	Inside pasterns	Lower outside wall; watch for contraction, sidebones, and corns on inside heel; square toe; and put lateral extension on inside
Calf-knees	Cannon bone angles forward from knee down	Whole knee area	Horse seldom remains sound under heavy work
Bucked-knees	Cannon bone angles back from knee down	Fetlock area	Often present at birth but disappears within 6 months or less
Knock-knees	Congenital or nutritional	Mostly inside knees	See veterinarian
Bowlegs	Congenital or nutritional	Mostly inside knees	See veterinarian
Off-set cannon bone—outside	Congenital	Inside splint bone	Weak conformation and inhibits free movement to some extent
Forward	Congenital	—	
Back	Congenital	—	
Standing under in front	Can be caused by sore hind feet		Heels may be too high
Camped in front	Can be caused by sore front feet if hind feet are well under body	Tendons and ligaments at rear of leg	Toes may be too long

CONFORMATION DEFECTS OF HIND LEGS

Defect	Cause	Effect on gait	Area under strain	Remarks	Horseshoer's correction
Base-narrow	Legs	Wings out	Outside of bones, ligaments, and joints	Often bowlegged—legs are straight to hock and then bend inward	Lower inside wall, use lateral extension on outside of toe, use trailer on outside branch if feet toe-in
Base-wide	Legs	Wings in may interfere	Inside of bones, ligaments, and joints	Most common form is cow-hocked	Lower outside wall, use lateral extension on inside, but bevel in underneath so it will not cut horse if he interferes
Cow-hocked	Legs	Wings in,	Inside of hock joint	Strain on hock may cause bone spavin, hind legs have tendency to go wide in sliding stop	Lower outside wall, (prevents worsening of defect in young horses), use lateral extension on inside of toe, swelled heel on inside branch

Sickle-hocked	Legs	Helps horse learn sliding stop	Rear of hock	If defect very pronounced, horse will probably not stand up under hard use—hock comes under great stress—makes horse subject to curb	Lower toe as much as possible, heel calk on inside branch may help if splayfooted
Straight (in back)	Legs		Front of hock	Makes horse subject to bog spavin and stifle, easily injured by heavy work, pasterns will be too straight	Lower heels as much as possible
Standing under	Same as sickle-hocked				Lower toe if too long
Camped behind	Legs			Horse will have upright pasterns	Lower heels if too high

ble, falter, and fall. If their conformation is such that they cannot be cured, it is best to get another horse. Remember that the front legs support, guide, and direct the power from the hind legs. If the front legs break down at high speed, you are in for a bad wreck.

XI

Special Shoeing

BULLS AND OXEN

SHOEING BULLS in rocky country can be one of the most economical things a rancher can do, although few cattle owners realize it. It will result in a higher percentage calf crop with fewer bulls needed, as a sore-footed bull is less active. It is expensive to keep a bull for a year, and, as fewer bulls are needed, the expense is less.

When a bull is shod, he must first be thrown or tied to a stout post with his head low and against a solid object. Two men can shoe a small bull without throwing him by using a pole put between his legs for leverage to lift the foot.

To tie a bull, take a nylon rope, slip the noose around his horns, take a half hitch around his chest (with the hitch on top), and another around his flank. Take the free end under his tail, then forward under the horn noose, and tie it to a post.

A large bull must be thrown since you cannot pick up his feet. To do this, tie the bull securely. Then take about 40 feet of good stout rope, double it, and tie a knot about two or three feet from the bight. Put this loop over his head with the knot resting on his brisket. Pass the ends of the rope between the forelegs. Carry each end around a hind leg just above the fetlock joint from the outside in and then under itself once. Bring the free ends forward, passing one end through each side of the neck loop. The free ends are taken to the rear of the bull and pulled by several men or riders. When the bull is down, the front and rear legs on each side are tied together and the rope used in throwing is removed.

It is best to keep the flank hitch ahead of the sheath or at least not to leave it tight for more than a few minutes. If there are cowboys around, they can team-tie the bull and save a lot of time and danger in putting on the foot ropes.

A simple method for trimming is to run the bull in a chute, put a strap under his chest, and lift him by using a tractor and a hydraulic lift. The bull will then usually be easy to handle.

Since a bull's hoofs have very thin walls, be careful not to drive the nails in too far. Small nails, such as No. 4 race-track nails, should be used, with five in each half-shoe. Use two clips, one over the inside of the toe and a smaller one on the outside. Calks can be used, if they are needed for surer footing; otherwise they should be left off completely. Each shoe is in two pieces (as shown in the accompanying illustration).

CITY HORSES

Horses used on hard streets or concrete, such as yard horses at stockyards, are being used in unnatural conditions, and their feet and legs must be taken care of

A

B

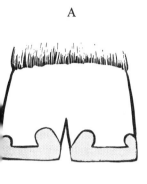
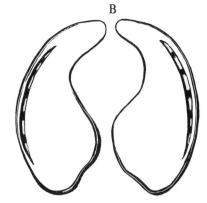

BULL SHOES

Bull hoof
(*showing clips*)

Bull shoes

as much as possible in order to keep these horses sound. Horses should never be run on the pavement as the shock to the bones and tendons is tremendous.

The feet should never be allowed to dry out as dryness increases the ill effects of concussion. Soak the feet overnight occasionally, and when they contain the proper amount of moisture, a hoof dressing may be used to prevent evaporation.

If it is necessary to work the horse exceptionally hard on concrete, a rubdown with a good leg wash afterward will add years to his life, and a good cooling out is always important.

When preparing the foot for the shoe, do not trim it quite as close as usual because the extra wall helps to dissipate concussion.

199

Plate shoes are preferred since they are the nearest thing to the natural hoof. A borium-treated shoe will give an exceptionally good grip on concrete and will prolong the life of the shoe (see "Hard-surfacing Shoes" in Chapter VII). Rubber shoes are manufactured which absorb the concussion. A piece of rubber inner tube, felt, or leather placed between the foot and shoe will help absorb some of the shock.

Draft Horses

When pulling a load, the horse does most of the work with his hind feet and legs. For this reason blunt toe and heel calks are used on the hind hoofs to give better footing. For ordinary work on average roads, use plate shoes on the forefeet. Some horses will stand better if they are harnessed while being shod, and a front foot can be tied to the hames. If two horses are members of a team, keep them where they can see each other as they are shod.

Generally heel and toe calks are used on shoes that are larger than size three, because horses with such large feet are used more for draft and slow work and do not require the speed and agility of the light horses. Here again, if there is no need for calks, don't use them.

Gaited Horses

By gaited horses, I mean the "high school" horses, usually American Saddle-bred, that are trained to do the artificial but graceful high-stepping gaits. They are classified as three- or five-gaited horses and their action is achieved by breeding, training, and shoeing.

200

Usually these horses are shod in an unnatural condition that strains both the flexor and extensor tendons, aggravates conformation weakness, and subjects the hoof to contraction. The proper rules of hoof care are sacrificed to satisfy someone's vanity. I am not in favor of this practice, but would like to examine the methods used, because, to a lesser extent, the same principles are used in everyday horseshoeing.

One trainer has said, "*After* the horse is trained to pick up his feet in the proper manner, weight may be added and the angle changed." This sounds like the proper way to do it, but if the horse can be trained to do these things, why alter his foot and add weight at all? The fact is, unfortunately, that in nearly all cases the toe is allowed to grow long and weight is added to achieve the training desired. However, if the horse is shod to pace, he could later be trained to rack.

The object is to increase the elevation of the front feet in action. There are several ways to do this, but the main principle involved is to delay the break-over, which increases the height of the foot during the first half of the stride.

The wall at the toe is encouraged to grow extremely long and/or pads are used under the shoe. Pads keep the old sole from sloughing off naturally, which helps to reinforce the long wall, but the sole also builds up around the frog, preventing its natural function. Added length on the hoof increases the length of the lower leg in relation to the upper leg, and this added length also increases momentum and, therefore, height of the stride. Sometimes, in order to increase the delaying effect, a piece of iron is welded across the shoe back from the toe. This is called a "Memphis bar." Heavy-toe-weighted shoes are generally used so that the effect of delaying the break-over plus inertia and the momentum of the added weight produces a high stride. Added weight usually increases length of the stride, but in this case the added weight causes energy to be expended in the upward lift instead of the forward swing, thus shortening the stride.

In addition to the above steps, which are artificial and harmful in themselves, a chain is sometimes fastened around the pastern. This hurts the horse as his foot strikes the ground and makes him snatch up his foot, increasing the snap at take-off and helping to keep this whole cycle in motion.

Since the wall is so long, a large nail, such as a No. 16, is used in order to get a grip in the live horn. A toe clip is often used to help hold the shoe, and it can be long and narrow to give a decorative effect. The inside edge of the shoe is often dished to help prevent forging. In my opinion, the weight would give a more desired effect if placed in the heels; the problem, however, is that the hind shoe might hit the enlarged heels. For this reason lead weights are sometimes screwed directly to the hoof.

HARNESS HORSES

I have had no experience shoeing harness horses, and what I write here is derived from other people. Standard-bred horses are most often used in harness.

These horses are shod differently depending on whether the owner wants them to trot or pace (see accompanying chart). Hoof angle and weight are the primary considerations. Heavy shoes on the forefeet help the horse trot because they increase the activity of the front quarters. Weight at the toe gives the horse a longer reach while weight at the heels helps the horse flex the knee and raise the heels higher. To make a trotter pace, use light shoes on the forefeet and heavy ones on the hind feet. The toe is sometimes lengthened on pacers to increase the length of stride.

The outside heels should be turned out slightly on a pacer. This pivots the toe to the outside as the hoof comes to rest and will help prevent cross-firing. Horses that toe-out in front and toe-in behind will have trouble with the pace. These horses should wear protective pads on their fetlocks and legs so that they do not hurt themselves.

Squaring the toe of the shoe makes the hoof break over in the center, and helps provide a straight line of flight. Lateral extensions and toe grabs also do this. If this shoe does not correct the action, a feathered-edge shoe or half-round shoe should be used (see "Interfering and Speedy Cutting" in Chapter X) so that there is less chance of damage to the leg if it is hit.

A smaller angle (lowering the heels) makes the foot rise higher during the first half of the stride and helps

Trot–Pace Chart

	Pace		Trot	
	Front	*Hind*	*Front*	*Hind*
Hoof angle	High	Low	Low	High
Shoe weight	Light	Heavy	Heavy	Light
Shoe length	Short	Long	Long	Short
Hoof length	Short	Long	Long	Short
Other	Rolled toe	Toe weight	Toe weight	Square toe

the horse trot. Generally, different weights, angles, and shapes are tried and the combination used that produces the best results.

ICE SHOES

There are many ways to give a horse footing on ice. If the shoe is fitted with sharp projections, there is danger that the horse will injure himself or other horses. This is the *only* time when toe calks are justified on a normal saddle horse.

Iron shoes draw the cold and could be a factor in freezing a horse's feet in extremely cold weather and deep snow. Usually only the frog or coronet is frozen, and a dry hard foot is less subject to freezing than a moist soft one.

Sometimes the shoes are pulled when the horse is not needed for a while and then tacked on with a couple of nails in each branch before he is used again. This "trip basis" method works well as you keep using the same holes.

Commercial ice shoes that have screw-in-type calks are available. The calks have a hardened core and last very well. These shoes will give as good a grip on ice as is possible to obtain, and when they are used with a rubber or leather pad under the shoe to keep the snow from balling up, the horse can move safely under almost any winter conditions. The calks should be removed if the horse is not to be used for a while and threaded plugs or cork should be inserted in the holes to keep them clean and free of burrs. If the horse is to be used regularly, the calks may be spot-welded in the shoe so that they are not lost. I would not weld them on in rocky country, however, as they will break off and new ones will need to be inserted. A better job of fitting can be done if these shoes are heated. The calks must be inserted before the shoe is bent or the holes will be stretched and the calks cannot be started. Always tighten the calks after the shoe is bent.

Taking pieces of rake teeth, roller bearings, or cutting pieces from a rasp and welding them to a regular shoe to make an ice shoe works well. An ordinary weld will help roughen the surface, a hard-surface weld is better, and borium is best because it has tungsten-carbide particles in the softer filler metal. As this wears away, it leaves the particles exposed, giving an excellent grip on ice or concrete. Borium may be applied either with an electric or gas welder, but gas works best. Half the borium used should be applied to the toe and one-fourth on each heel for even wear (see "Hard-surfacing Shoes" in Chapter VII).

If no hard-surface rod is available, take a piece of cast iron and heat it until it starts to melt. Rub this on the white-hot shoe or calk to be hardened and then plunge it into water to cool and harden.

Ordinary calks may be heated and sharpened. The outside calk should be sharpened crossways and the inside one sharpened at right angles to the toe and set well under the shoe so that there is less chance of the horse's treading on himself. Tread wounds of the coronet are especially bad as this is the area that produces the new horn. After the calks are sharpened, they may be hard-surfaced to stay sharp longer. Harden only the outside so that the inside will wear away and keep the calk sharp. Although the screw-calk ice shoe gives as good a grip as is possible to obtain, these shoes are cheaper, easier to fit, and safer for both the horse wearing them and other horses. There is no problem with lost calks and no special tools are necessary.

Frost nails are a good way to provide temporary footing. These nails have long, sharp heads. Several of the regular nails can be removed and these nails inserted to give a good grip on ice. If these nails are to be used, special holes with an outward pitch can be punched in the shoe near the ends of the branches. The nails may then be driven through the shoe without entering the hoof, or only the very edge, and bent over the shoe.

Frost nails can be made by hard-surfacing the heads of regular nails while they are hot. Bend half of them so the heads are at right angles and use a size larger than the nails holding the shoe so that the heads will stick up.

Rounding the inner border of the shoe will give some help in keeping snow from balling up in the foot. If nothing else is available, filling the horse's foot with grease may be enough to get you home.

There are special rubber pads to prevent snow from balling. For a foot with a very large frog, rubber is better than a thick leather pad, as it has more give to it and can more easily make the bend where it goes over the frog and under the shoe. Give is important because a very large frog could be crushed and cause overexpansion. Other materials such as belting and rubber from an inner tube may be used, and will work very well.

206

Put a ball of pine tar and oakum in the center of the foot before putting on the rubber. The resulting bulge is very effective in keeping out snow. It also acts as an artificial frog if the real frog is small. The pine tar acts as a germicide and prevents evaporation through the sole.

When putting on a pad, fit the shoe to the hoof, nail the pad to the shoe with a nail on each side, cut off the nails even with the pad, and trim the pad to fit the shoe. Now nail the shoe on and pull out the nails holding the pad in place. A pad should always be packed, and if oakum is not available, burlap will do.

When the weather is extremely cold, snow isn't much of a problem; but when it warms up enough for snow to ball, the problem can become so acute that a horse cannot be used unless something is done to prevent balling. Often only the front feet are shod with a pad since a horse snaps his hind feet a little more and can kick the balls out of them better. Trying to use a horse when his feet are packed with snow can result in strains and sprains because his foot has no support. An unshod horse with the walls trimmed won't have as much trouble.

In my opinion, the commercial ice shoes have the toe calks set too close together. If you are making an ice shoe, try welding the toe nail holes shut and setting the calks over them. This gives more lateral support to the toe, and since the calks are not so close together, the snow does not ball up behind them as badly. Since setting the calks in this manner will make the foot break over slightly quicker, you may not want to treat the hind shoes this way. Speeding up the front feet is a good idea because a horse lunging in deep snow has a tendency to tear his front shoes off with the hind ones, and this method helps to get the front feet out of the way.

If the coronet is injured—and the most common causes of coronet injuries are calks and barbed wire—use a bar shoe and lower the wall under the cut. This will reduce movement and concussion and aid in healing. Bag balm is very good for these injuries. If the sharp-shod horse has a tendency to kick other horses, he should be kept in a corral by himself.

MULES

When handling mules, never allow them to get the better of you, even in little things. Make them understand from the start that you are the boss. Mules are smarter than horses, and they will not put themselves into a position where they are likely to get hurt. Mules are good workers if ruled with a firm hand, and sometimes a firm grip on a club. I guess their long ears make them absent-minded and sometimes you have to get their attention first. Use this "Indian lovin'" on his rump, not his head. When an airplane stalls you don't take a hammer to the propeller, do you?

Mules are club-footed; in other words, they have a narrow, stumpy foot. The buttresses are not even with the bulbs of the frog as in a horse's foot. Fit the shoe so that the branch extends beyond the buttress at least to a point even with the bulbs of the frog. Turn the heel calks out slightly to give lateral support to the narrow foot. When driving nails, it may be necessary to bend the tips outward slightly (flat side) before they are driven so that they will come out at the right height, especially heel nails.

The sole of a mule's foot is quite concave, and does not become tender as fast as that of his flatter-footed cousins. If mules are not worked hard, they may not need to be shod at all. Mule shoes are the same for front and hind feet.

PARADE HORSES

A special shoe called a "Scotch Parade" shoe can be made for these horses. It has a large toe clip and the angle of the outside of the branch is the same as that of the wall. The surface is then ground and polished or even brazed and polished to a bronze color.

This is an excellent shoe for a high-stepping parade horse or show stud, but it takes a lot of skill to make. Once a set is made, it can be kept for special occasions.

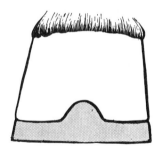

SCOTCH PARADE SHOE

Note: Angle of the shoe corresponds to that of the wall.

Ordinary shoes may be polished or painted to give a flashy step. Use plastic wood to fill in any cracks or broken-out wall.

RACE HORSES

Here again I have no experience, but I will list everything I have found out about shoeing race horses in order to make this book as complete as possible.

Steel plates are generally used for training, and light steel or aluminum shoes are put on just before a race. These light shoes may be purchased with or without nail holes. Holes may be punched cold and put in or added wherever needed. Heating these aluminum shoes in hot water makes them easier to bend, and they can be bent with a copper or wood hammer. The branches of aluminum shoes may be tied together with sheet metal and copper rivets. This may be necessary for a flat-footed horse with a lot of expansion in the heels. Before nailing an aluminum shoe to the leveled foot, make sure that there is a little space under each branch. It will close as the nails are driven, and the heels will be tight.

Heels are usually lowered as much as practical to give the horse a longer stride, but lowering the heels below the natural angle is, no doubt, a contributing factor to tendon injuries, especially in colts.

A full-swedge shoe is almost always used (crease runs completely around the shoe). The shoe may be adapted in many ways, but cannot exceed certain rules which vary with different tracks. Generally a toe grab is used for grip and leverage. Block heels, stickers, jar calks, and mud inserts are also used. One type of toe grab, called the "Louisiana toe grab," is bent forward from the bottom of the toe and really gives a running horse an advantage with its extra leverage; however, it has been banned at many tracks. A horse could easily cut his flexor tendons or injure another horse with this type of shoe.

Race track farriers generally use a small "stall jack," which may be driven into the ground, instead of an anvil, and it is all that is required for fitting aluminum shoes.

When exercising race horses, especially colts, it is better for their legs if they are run both ways around the track, since always running in the same direction can lead to trouble.

Rodeo Horses

The main points to remember when shoeing rodeo horses are to use light weight, good steel, and full-swedge shoes.

There are several good types on the market at the present time. Polo plates are good, although the inner rim is high, and a shoe with a high outer rim gives a slightly greater amount of leverage. Polo shoes should not be used for a calf-roping horse's hind feet because the rim has a tendency to stop the foot from sliding and could result in injury to the fetlock area. There is a special roping shoe with trimmed heels to aid the sliding stop.

Hoof angle becomes very important when shoeing rodeo horses since they must have speed and agility. A foot gauge should be used so that the angle and length of toe are exactly the same for corresponding feet. A small angle will help a horse shoot his feet under him; a larger angle will allow the foot to break over faster.

These horses should always be shod short and fine on the front feet. In other words, the shoe should stop at the end of the wall and not hang over. If it projects, the hind feet can catch the front shoes as the horse lunges out of the box, tearing them off. The rodeo horse will have to be reshod more often than the average horse as the shoe grows forward and soon will not support the rear of the foot as it should.

A small trick, if the horse is wearing regular keg shoes, is to heat the toe and complete the crease around the toe for a little better grip, or another groove may be made behind the first one.

A special shoe can be made for a horse when training for the sliding stop. The shoe is made of 1 1/2-inch by 5/16-inch iron, the toe is rocked, and the heels are "spooned" out (flattened and bent up). The heavy shoe helps the horse shoot his feet under him, and the wide heels help the slide and protect the heels. Use a regular shoe on the forefeet.

If the arena is muddy, a properly shod horse can win everything in sight. Pull his regular shoes and put on light shoes with very thin calks or "stickers." A leather pad can be used under the shoe. Then the pad and the whole foot can be smeared with grease and covered with a sack until just before the horse's run so that the mud will not ball up on his feet. A little extra work may mean several hundred dollars at the pay window.

If a rope horse is cow-hocked, the hind feet will have a tendency to go wide as he shoots them under his body. A short calk under the inside heel will help to make the foot slide straight.

XII.

Horseshoes
and Horse Traders

Ride the horse before you buy it." This is sound advice, but in addition to trying the horse and observing his conformation and disposition, you will want to check him for soundness.

There are many ways of hiding unsoundness, and an unscrupulous dealer won't hesitate to use them. If you plan to buy a horse from this kind of individual, it may be best not to let him know when you are coming to inspect the horse so he cannot give it pain pills or a shot ahead of time.

Trying out a horse is one time you can use him hard on a hard surface as this may make any unsoundness apparent. Defects of the feet and legs are those most often hidden, but you should make sure the horse's eyes and teeth are sound, too.

It is a good idea to try the horse while he is unshod, making allowance for a natural tenderness. Shoes can hide a multitude of sins, including a slight case of founder, corns, and defects of gait. High heels are a common way of covering spavin and tendon disorders. On the other hand, normal shoes that show wear may be a

214

good indication that the horse has been used, and this is what you want. There should be no extensions or trailers on the shoes, and they should be worn evenly. If one area is worn low, either the shoes have been put on wrong or the horse is sore and favoring the high side.

Observe the legs from the front, side, and back, watching for bumps and comparing each leg with the opposite one. Now feel each leg. On the hind legs, pay particular attention to the hock area, especially the inside. On the front legs, check the inside of the cannon bone for splints and the pasterns for ringbones. These growths can occur anywhere in the pastern area. The area at the top and sides of the hoof should be fairly pliable if the lateral cartilages are normal and no side bones are present.

Besides feeling for enlargements, feel for soft areas that could indicate windpuffs and also for areas that are warm or insensitive to the touch. Practice feeling the legs of a sound horse so that you will be able to recognize an unsound one.

XIII.

Highlight Summary

Rules of Gait

1. To speed break-over, shorten the stride, and vice versa.
2. A long toe retards break-over, decreases elevation, and lengthens stride.
3. A square-toed shoe shortens the stride slightly because the foot breaks over quicker.
4. Long heels brake the foot slightly as it lands, shorten the stride, and reduce speed.
5. A rocker toe quickens break-over, increases height, shortens stride, and reduces concussion.
6. On a sidehill, feet wing downhill.
7. The low side of a crooked hoof carries most of the weight because it is closer to the correct line of stance.

Some Basic Shoeing Rules

1. In a crooked hoof lower the "side that points" from the toe to heel and leave the other heel high.
2. Use the lightest shoe that will allow the horse to do the job he is intended for.

216

3. Use a plate shoe unless you have reason to do otherwise.

4. A bar shoe gives maximum support for healing, and can be made to give extra frog pressure or no frog pressure.

5. If you use a projection, put a clip on that side.

6. If the outside of the hoof wears heavily, set the shoe wide on the outside. If the heels wear heavily, shoe the horse long.

7. Pritchel the way the nail is driven so no burr is left in the hole to cut the nail.

8. If the horse is used on rutted roads, point the toe as much as possible so the foot can break over either side.

9. Don't cut too low at the quarters. Start the cut at the low heel.

10. Don't use weight to solve problems if it can be done some other way.

11. Don't apply greasy hoof dressing until *after* the hoof is soaked.

General Hints

1. If the sole starts to bleed, lay a small piece of horn over it and apply heat to cauterize and stop the bleeding.

2. Use an electric heating pad to apply heat.

3. Develop skill with the nippers in order to avoid rasping.

4. Carry nails in one pant's cuff and stubs in the other.

5. A good rule is to "measure twice and cut once."

217

6. An electric vibrator is a good method of massage.
7. To apply cold water when needed, mount a tank above the horse in the stall and fill it with iced water. Bandage the area to be treated with a thick, flannel bandage and run a small rubber hose from the tank under the bandage so that gravity causes the water to feed into it.

PRACTICAL HORSE CARE

1. Keep the feet moist.
2. Let the horse go bare when you can.
3. Avoid concussion as much as possible. This means a slow gait on a hard surface.
4. When possible, avoid running a horse up or down-hill.
5. Pull the shoes and trim the feet closely in the fall so that snow will not ball up in the long feet and the hoofs will not be broken out in the spring when it is time to reshoe.
6. Put bell boots on a horse shod with calks before hauling him so he doesn't injure himself, or if there is a chance other horses might step on him.
7. Check with a veterinarian at the first sign of lameness.
8. Set up a schedule for your horse so that he receives the shots he needs and is wormed regularly. Since tetanus bacteria are so common in horse manure, it is a good idea to vaccinate the horse and give him a booster shot each year.
9. Don't expect too much of the horse when he is out of shape. Regular exercise is good and absolutely

necessary if he must do some hard work. Otherwise the horse can "go sore," and will not be useful at all.

10. In freezing weather warm the bit by holding it in your hand, or use a hackamore. In hot weather you may need to cool the bit before putting it in the horse's mouth if it has been hanging in the sun.

11. To avoid broken bridle reins and a sore mouth, learn to ride the horse with a rope around his neck. Use an eight-foot piece of soft nylon. Tie this snugly around his neck in a bowline when you catch him and never take it off until he is turned loose. Tuck the free end in your belt when mounting the horse or tie a slip knot over the horn. Before dismounting, take the rope in your left hand, leaving the reins over the horn. Use this rope to tie the horse.

12. Always warm the horse up before hard use and cool him out afterward.

13. Avoid barbed wire and never tie a horse to a wire fence. More horses are ruined by wire than anything else.

14. A good horseman takes care of his horse before he takes care of himself.

15. After a hard ride, never jerk the saddle off right away or the horse's back will swell. The blood has been pressed out during the ride so loosen the cinches, letting the blood come back slowly.

16. Don't turn a shod horse out with a halter on.

17. Of general interest to horsemen are the growths on the inside of horses' legs often called "chest-nuts." These growths are normal and their real

name is "callosities." If the light is right and you look into the horse's eyes, you will see some growths; these too are normal. They are called *copora nigra* or "black bodies."

CONCLUSION

Well, here it is; I've come to the end of my yarn. This subject of horses' feet and shoeing is such a big one that I hardly feel I've made a dent in it. I hope it has stimulated your interest and given you a desire to learn more.

You might say this book is "fresh from the anvil." I made notes as I worked, then put them together at night and in the winter when there wasn't much shoeing to do.

I am sure there are better methods in many cases than the ones I have described here, but I would say, in general, do it this way until you find a better one.

Best wishes—when you get to the end of your rope, tie a knot in it and HANG ON!

The Village Blacksmith

Under a spreading Chestnut-tree
    The village smithy stands;
The smith, a mighty man is he,
    With large and sinewy hands;
And muscles of his brawny arms
    Are strong as iron bands.

His hair is crisp, and black, and long,
    His face is like the tan;
His brow is wet with honest sweat,
    He earns what'er he can,
And looks the whole world in the face,
    For he owes not any man.

Week in, week out, from morn till night,
    You can hear his bellows blow;
You can hear him swing his heavy sledge,
    With measured beat and slow,
Like a sexton ringing the village bell,
    When the evening sun is low.

And children coming home from school
    Look in at the open door;
They love to see the flaming forge,
    And hear the bellows roar,
And catch the burning sparks that fly
    Like chaff from a threshing-floor.

He goes on Sunday to the church,
    And sits among his boys;
He hears the parson pray and preach,
    He hears his daughter's voice,
Singing in the village choir,
    And it makes his heart rejoice.

221

It sounds to him like her mother's voice,
    Singing in Paradise!
He needs must think of her once more,
    How in the grave she lies;
And with his hard, rough hand he wipes
    A tear out of his eyes.

Toiling, rejoicing, sorrowing,
    Onward through life he goes;
Each morning sees some task begun,
    Each evening sees it close;
Something attempted, something done,
    Has earned a night's repose.
Thanks, thanks to thee, my worthy friend,
    For the lesson thou hast taught!
Thus at the flaming forge of life
    Our fortunes must be wrought;
Thus on its sounding anvil shaped
    Each burning deed and thought.

—Henry Wadsworth Longfellow

Bibliography

Adams, O. R. *Lameness in Horses*. Philadelphia, Lea & Febiger, 1962.

Davenport, C. *The Foot and Shoeing*. London, The British Horse Society, 2d ed., 1962.

Frank, E. R. *Veterinary Surgery*. Minneapolis, Burgess Publishing Co., 1953.

Holmes, Charles M. *Principles and Practice of Horseshoeing*. Leeds, England, The Farrier's Journal Publishing Co., Ltd., 1949.

Holmestrom, J. G. *Modern Blacksmithing and Horseshoeing*. Chicago, Frederick J. Drake & Co., 1913.

Hunting, William. *The Art of Horse-Shoeing*. London, Bailliere, Tindal and Cox, 1922.

Jefferson, T. B., and Gorham Woods. *Metals and How to Weld Them*. Cleveland, James F. Lincoln Arc Welding Foundation, 2d ed., 1965.

Kays, D. J. *The Horse*. New York, Rinehart & Co., 1959.

Kimbel, Ken. *Horseshoes of Interest to Veterinarians*. Plant City, Florida, 1946 ed.

Knowles, Charles N. *Care of Horses' Legs and Corrective Horseshoeing*. San Luis Obispo, California State Polytechnic College, AH90-a, 1963.

Kuger, Harold. *Arc Welding Lessons for School and Farm Shop*. Cleveland, James F. Lincoln Arc Welding Foundation, 2d ed., 1965.

223

La Croix, J. V. *Lameness of the Horse*. Chicago, *American Journal of Veterinary Medicine*, 1916.

Lungwitz, A. and J. W. Adams. *A Textbook of Horseshoeing*. Philadelphia, J. B. Lippincott Co., 1913.

Miller, William C. and Geoffrey P. West. *Encyclopedia of Animal Care*. Baltimore, The Williams & Wilkins Co., 7th ed., 1964.

Reeks, H. C. *Diseases of the Horse's Foot*. Chicago, Alexander Eger, 1906.

Russell, William. *Scientific Horseshoeing*. Cincinnati, C. J. Krenbiel & Co., 1907.

Savage, H. M. *Evolution of the Horseshoe*. Veterinary Bulletin, supplement to the Army Medical Bulletin, Vol. 6, No. 2, November 24, 1920.

Selvidge, R. W., and J. M. Allton. *Blacksmithing*. Peoria, Illinois, Manual Arts Press, 1925.

Troy Chemical Company. *Hoof Care*. Port Chester, New York, 1962.

Troy Chemical Company. *How to Determine and Treat Lameness and Unsoundness in Horses*. New York, 41st ed., 1961.

U.S. Department of Agriculture. *Diseases of the Horse*. Washington, D.C., G.P.O., 1942.

U.S. War Department. *The Horseshoer*. Manual No. 2-220, Washington, D.C., G.P.O., 1941.

Western Horseman, The. *Horseshoeing and Hoof Care*. Colorado Springs, 1960.

Glossary

ANKYLOSIS: Term used when the bone surfaces of a joint grow together, making the joint immovable. A cast is applied for this purpose.

ANNEALING: Softening metal by the use of heat.

ANTIPHLOGISTIC PACKS: Medicine used to reduce inflammation; commonly used after hot and cold applications.

AZOTURIA: Commonly called "Monday morning sickness," a disease affecting horses on full feed without exercise.

BAR SHOE: Shoe with no opening between the heels; there are many variations.

BAREFOOT: Unshod

BELL BOOTS: Bell-like rubber protectors fastened around the pastern and covering the hoof.

BIGHT: The loop in a doubled rope.

BLANKS: Used here to refer to unfinished horseshoes that are fitted by heating them in the forge.

BREAK-OVER: Point in the stride when the foot leaves the ground, heels first, and starts its path of flight, preferably over the center of the toe.

BUFFER: Also called a clinch cutter; used to cut or straighten the nail clinches prior to removing the shoe.

BURR: Any small piece of iron in or over a nail hole that should be removed before nailing the shoe on.

225

CALK: Projection on the bottom of a horseshoe.

CHAMFERED: Having the surface hammered so that it. slopes.

CLINCH: Small portion of the nail that is bent over where it emerges through the hoof wall.

CLIP: Earlike projection anywhere along the outside edge of the foot surface of the shoe.

CLOSE NAIL: Nail driven so close to the sensitive tissues that it puts pressure on them without actually penetrating.

CLUBFOOTED: Having a narrow, stumpy foot.

COKE: Substance that remains and is burned in the forge after the gases have been driven from the coal.

CORTICOSTEROID: Drug that causes a suppression of inflammation; cannot be used when infection is present.

CREASE: Also called a "fullering groove"; the depression in the ground surface of the shoe, in which nail holes are located.

DOG FASHION: Term used to indicate that the horse's body is slanted to one side as he moves because a leg, or legs, is taking a shorter stride than the opposite leg.

DUBBED OFF: Hoof has been rasped off on top to fit a shoe that was not bent to fit the hoof.

EXTENSION: Projection on the shoe, usually on one side of the toe.

FARRIER: Person skilled in the art of horseshoeing; may or may not also be a blacksmith.

FINE: Shoe is fitted closely and narrow and does not extend beyond the hoof at the heels or quarters.

FOOT SURFACE: Surface of the shoe that touches the hoof wall.

FROST NAILS: Special hardened nails that protrude above the shoe to provide grip.

FULL: Shoe is fitted liberally and wide and may extend beyond the wall at the heels or quarters.

FULL ROLLER SHOE: Outside edge of the ground surface has been rounded.

FULL SWEDGE: Crease that runs completely around the shoe.

GRAB: Projection on the ground surface of the shoe, placed in the toe area and used for leverage and in some cases to make the foot break over the toe.

GROUND SURFACE: Surface of the shoe that touches the ground.

HACKAMORE: Headstall with a nosepiece but no bit inside the horse's mouth.

HAMES: Frames that fit over the neck collar of the harness.

HANDMADE SHOE: Shoe made by hand from a piece of iron; see blanks.

"HEART BAR" SHOE: Shoe with bar widened in the center in the shape of a heart.

HIGH SIDE: Side of the hoof wall that is grown highest; foot points to this side.

HORN: Insensitive wall of the horse's hoof.

KEG SHOE: Ready-made shoes used in cold shoeing.

LEATHER FILLERS: Pieces of leather nailed or bolted to the shoe to balance the hoof or put pressure on the frog.

LOW SIDE: Side of the hoof wall that is short.

MILD STEEL: Iron containing up to .30% carbon; material used in most horseshoes.

ONE-SIDED: Characteristic of horses making it necessary to train them on both sides since they have difficulty in transferring what they have learned from one side to the other.

OSSIFICATION: Deposit of calcium and other substances on bone or cartilage; caused by inflammation resulting from concussion or injury; calcification.

PLATE SHOE: Flat shoe with no projections on the ground surface.

POINT: Holding hoof in such a position that only the toe contacts the ground.

POULTICE: Soft mass of bran or other material containing a medication and applied to an injured area.

PREDISPOSED: Tending or susceptible to.

ROCKED TOE: Toe of the shoe is bent up.

ROLLED TOE: Toe of the shoe has outside edge of ground surface rounded off.

SEATING OUT: Act of hammering down the inside of the foot surface while shoe is hot.

SHIMS: Material inserted between two surfaces to prevent excess movement.

SOAK STALL: Stall or pen with a moist floor where horses can be confined so their hoofs will absorb moisture.

SPOONED: Heels of shoe are flattened and bent up.

SUTURE: Sewing or a stitch.

SWEENY: Term used when muscles disappear; caused by lack of use because of pain or injury to the nerves.

SWELLED HEELS: Heels that have been thickened, normally by turning under the ends of the branches and then welding them to the branches.

TENDOVAGINITIS: Telescoping of the sheath surrounding the flexor tendons when it is torn from its attachments; common in race horses.

TENOTOMY: Division of a tendon performed by surgery.

TRAILER: Elongation of a branch, usually turned out at an angle.

TURNED HEELS: Ends of the branches are bent down at right angles to form a calk.

TWYER (tuyère) BALL: Slotted ball in the forge that holds the coal but allows air to enter the fire.

228

WAR BRIDLE: Device to control the horse while he is being held.

WING: Foot moving in a horizontal arc, either in or out.

Index

232